HORROR
AND
THE HOLY

HORROR AND THE HOLY

Wisdom-Teachings of the Monster Tale

Kirk J. Schneider

OPEN COURT
Chicago and La Salle, Illinois

✸

OPEN COURT and the above logo are registered in the U.S. Patent and Trademark Office.

First printing 1993

Printed and bound in the United States of America.

Library of Congress Cataloging-in-Publication Data
Schneider, Kirk J.
    Horror and the holy : wisdom-teachings of the monster tale / Kirk
J. Schneider.
        p.   cm.
    Includes bibliographical references (p.) and index.
    ISBN 0-8126-9224-1. — ISBN 0-8126-9225-X (pbk.)
    1. Horror tales—History and criticism. 2. Holy, The, in
literature. 3. Literature—Psychology.   I. Title.
PN3435.S36 1993   93-3634
809.3'8738—dc20   CIP

To Jūratė

Contents

List of Illustrations

Preface

I am sitting in a dark theater watching David Cronenberg's *The Fly*. Suddenly, I am struck by my fascination. How could I, a relatively temperate individual, be so fixated on the grisly events before me? How could the hundred or so patrons in the theater with me be equally entranced? How can there be so much *prurient* interest in general?

Then it dawns on me. We are all so captivated because there are elements of the sacred in what we witness. There is an intersection here between horror and the holy! Creation, destruction, the monstrous—each of these touch on the extraordinary as well as on the pathological.

Why else would so many of us be attracted to dangerous or extreme situations—carnivals, bloodsports, mountain climbing, sex palaces, military battles? Why else would we be captivated by crime, mayhem, and cataclysm? Even in ancient times, biblical writers understood our enchantment with the macabre.

But there is another reason for our fixation on the horrific: horror provides us with a view of one of the fundamental human dilemmas—that which frees us versus that which limits us. We can *attempt* virtually anything, the genre stresses, but we must ever be apprised of the costs.

Certainly, I am not the only one to have made this observation. Some of us have made it intuitively, and others, like the author H. P. Lovecraft, have alluded to it explicitly.[1] A few psychologists—Freudians and Jungians mainly—have also made such observations but with moderately different emphases. None of these standpoints, however, has proved satisfactory to me. Either they treat the subject too briefly, as in Lovecraft's essay, or they don't quite grasp the profundity of the phenomenon, as in Freudian and Jungian considerations.

This book, then, is written for all those who see more in horror's unsettling domains. It is written for both academic and lay readers who perceive something momentous in classic horror, but who cannot find sourcebooks which fully legitimate this perception. Accordingly, *Horror and the Holy* opens with four psychological assumptions (which draw in part on earlier research I have published[2]): (1) classic horror (and by analogy the self/cosmic relation) is both ecstatic and terrifying; (2) the basis for this condition is infinity (or "the holy"); (3) the further we pursue the ecstatic, the more we unveil its terrifying context; and (4) the *encounter* with this context (as opposed to the denial or passive acceptance of this context) promotes vitality and social sensitivity.

After elaborating on the structure of these assumptions and their relevance to eleven classic tales, we explore their implications for living. Specifically, we consider their pertinence to psychological, social, scientific, and spiritual well-being. We close, finally, with a comment on the productive and unproductive dimensions of "evil."

One last note: To a large extent, I arrived at a spiritual understanding of life through horror—*my own* as well as that which I witnessed in books and movies. Although this may not be the traditional path to such a sensibility, it is a much more common one, I believe, than is ordinarily acknowledged. (Witness, for example, the phenomena of shamanism and the "wounded healer.") I hope that others, who are similarly disposed, can derive benefit from this perspective and from the exalted sentiments of Hölderlin: "Where danger is, the delivering power grows too."[3]

Acknowledgments

First and foremost, I am indebted to Don Cooper, whose wisdom, knowledge of film, and spirited conversations on horror have assisted me immeasurably. I am also grateful to J. A. Bricker, who thoroughly and perceptively reviewed this work in its early stages. My deepest appreciation, furthermore, to all those who have assisted me in emerging from my own horrors, and who have diversely modeled inspiring paths—among these: Edward Schiff, Ann Gustin, Debbie Hazelton, Don Rice, Jim Bugental, Rollo May, Stanley Krippner, and Sam Haramis, to name only a few. My heartfelt gratitude, finally, for the warm support of family and friends.

Niagara Falls (1969). Photo by Algimantas Kezys.

Introduction—Ecstasy, Terror, and Infinity

For beauty is . . . but the beginning of terror, which we . . . are just able to endure.

—RAINER MARIA RILKE

Infinity—and I mean here infinity of the small as well as the large—has ever held humanity in its sway. From the dawn of civilization, we have been fascinated by endlessness (or the *intimations* of endlessness). Cave drawings reveal immense beasts of prey. Ancient temples swell with excesses—giant pillars, dazzling spires, extravagant offerings to the gods. Obscure details have also been significant. Wind, rain, and snow are enduring objects of worship. The occult—darkness, phantoms, alchemy—has constantly intrigued us. The subtle world of microorganisms has never ceased to amaze.

Religiosity, love, poetry, art—these too celebrate the limitless (or what is believed to be limitless). We revel in them, become dizzy, giddy, intoxicated through them. Religions promise to immortalize us. Lovers create paradise. Poets and artists show us possibilities. We can cover the whole range with these vehicles, or so it seems. We can know total surrender and total dominance. We can give in, diminish, merge; and we can assert, expand, engulf.

But there is a hitch to our celebrations of the infinite (or the holy, in the classic sense of the term).[1] This is the other message that has been foretold. Celebration is joyful, this tradition suggests, but it is only partial; it is only the initial phase of what can be. On the other side terror reigns.[2] *Ecstasy is a glimpse of the infinite; terror is full disclosure.* Ecstasy is marked by a degree of

1

comfort, innocence, illusion; terror is ultimately bereft of these. Ecstasy implies some degree of containment or manageability; terror is unbridled. It is fine to say with Lao Tzu and the institutional Jesus that they are "the way," but the call of the tragedian, I believe, is more germane: "All [is] in doubt."[3]

The chief assumptions of this book, accordingly, are: (1) the basis for terror and ecstasy is infinity (or the holy); (2) terror sets the upper limit on ecstasy and not the other way around; and (3) the *encounter* with this limit promotes vitality and social sensitivity.

While the artistic, literary, and philosophical validations of our position are notable,[4] one relevant area—the horror tale— has been woefully underinvestigated. Daunting though it may be, horror slashes through life's surfaces and exposes the heart of our condition. It cuts through all of our comforts, from the obvious to the sublime, and unveils our *rootlessness*. At the same time, it suggests a way to *handle* this rootlessness.

For the balance of this book, we will pursue the horror phenomenon. First, we will consider the psychological structure of horror—how it arises, what it implies about ecstasy, how it relates to infinity. Next, we will consider the wisdom in horror beginning with two archetypal thrillers, *Dracula* and *Frankenstein*. Third, we will elaborate upon this wisdom with nine classic counterparts to the above—*The Phantom of the Opera*, "The Fall of the House of Usher," *The Invisible Man*, *The Incredible Shrinking Man*, *Dr. Jekyll and Mr. Hyde*, *The Birds*, *Forbidden Planet*, *Vertigo*, and *Alien*. Finally, we will consider horror as a worldview —what the moral and psychological lessons of horror are and how they can promote well-being.

Untitled artwork by Angela Campbell of the National Institute of Art and Disabilities, Richmond, California.

Part I
The Structure of Horror: Chaos and Obliteration

Whoso takes this survey of himself will be terrified at the thought that he is upheld . . . between these two abysses of the infinite and nothing, he will tremble at the sight of these marvels.

—Blaise Pascal

In order to understand horror, we must begin with "deviation."[1] Although deviation can also imply ecstasy, such deviation is *transitory*. The prospect of *unabating* deviation, on the other hand, is horrifying. This point can be illustrated by a simple vignette. If I take a mild sedative, I am likely to feel relaxed; if I take a few sedatives I will probably feel serene; if I overdose on sedatives, I will quite rapidly feel *immobilized*. To illustrate further—the early stages of love can be a joyful, intoxicating experience. But what happens when one lover becomes obsessed? What happens if this lover follows his partner around, can't stop thinking about her, and petitions her incessantly?

Now let us carry these cases further and contemplate *unceasing* sedation or *boundless* adoration. For example, what might it be like if we *could not stop* relaxing, if even death could not bar us from this process? What might such deterioration look like? Is it even conceivable? What about our *boundlessly* devoted lover? What if he followed his beloved *everywhere*? What if he clung to her *interminably*?

If these extremities strike a chord for you, then you have probably entered the world of horror. This is the world of the nightmare and the grotesque. What makes this world so disturbing is not merely its lethality (which might actually be welcomed under the circumstances!) but its *unstoppability*, its *endlessness*.

Take almost any deviation from customary experience, stretch it far enough, and you produce horror. Think about vision, for example. Observing the details of nature with normal, healthy eyes is a wondrous event. However, what if our eyes were capable of microscopic discriminations? What if we could see the details of common houseflies? What if we could peer into the molecular structure of food or skin? What if our entire visual field constituted microbes and electro-magnetic charges? By the same token, what if we could see into distant homes, towns, or even countries with a single glance? What if unaided visibility extended to other planets or solar systems? How manageable would our lives be?

This conception can be applied to *any* of our senses. Consider *unimpeded* hearing or *unlimited* physical sensation. What if we were bombarded with distant sounds or uncontrollable pain? The problem holds for thoughts and emotions as well. Contemplate *unbounded* anger, sadness, or envy. Consider *endless* analyzing, categorizing, or speculating. To be sure, writers use such exaggerated phraseology but only for dramatic effect. Reflect upon what such experiences might *literally* be like.

Even so-called elated states of consciousness can become harrowing. Heaven, Paradise, Nirvana—all of these *sound* beautiful. But what might they *actually* be like? How do *eternal* submission or *unceasing* harmony strike us? What about *perpetual* enthusiasm? Mark Twain (1962) has mused widely on these problems:

> In man's heaven *everybody sings!* The man who did not sing on earth sings there; the man who could not sing on earth is able to do it there. This universal singing is not casual, not occasional, not relieved by intervals of quiet; it goes on all day long . . . every day. . . .
>
> Meantime, every person is playing a harp. . . . Consider the deafening hurricane of sound—millions and millions of voices screaming at once and millions and millions of harps gritting their teeth at the same time! I ask you: is it hideous, is it odious, is it horrible? (pp. 10–11)

Deviation from the familiar, then, prompts discomfort. Extreme deviation, on the other hand, or what I term "contradiction," prompts *horror*. That which begins as a cure for nervousness, for example, winds up as *paralyzing*. That which starts as a casual fling ends in *obsession*. That which is initially wondrous turns *monstrous*. These are the earmarks of horror.

But we cannot stop here. Contradiction taken to its logical conclusion brings us to *infinity*. Why infinity? Because, as we have seen, the more a thing differs, the less manageable it becomes; the less manageable it becomes, the greater its linkage to extremity, obscurity, and, ultimately, *endlessness*.

Elsewhere, I have shown that human consciousness is characterized by two potentially endless poles—the *constrictive* and the *expansive* (Schneider 1990). Constrictive experience is typified by "drawing back" and confining; expansive perception is marked by "bursting forth" and extending. Many if not most of our horrors can be understood in this vein. Our "sedation" episode, for example, illustrates uncontrollable contraction; the "love" vignette suggests unmanageable extension (e.g., envelopment), as well as some contractive elements (e.g., obsession). Constriction is associated with a variety of states: retreating, diminishing, isolating, falling, emptying, or slowing. Expansion is linked to gaining, enlarging, dispersing, ascending, filling, or accelerating.

Now if we apply this model to horror classics, central themes become more intelligible. Is it any wonder that the genre is preoccupied by immensity, materialization, and explosiveness on the one hand, and imperceptibility, dematerialization, and entrapment on the other? And we must go even further. Superlative horror carries these dimensions to their ultimate point; it displays expansion and constriction in their starkest light. What, then, are the final implications of maximization (immensity, materialization, explosiveness) and minimization (imperceptibility, dematerialization, entrapment)? While we certainly cannot provide definitive answers here, my research suggests two polar eventualities—those of chaos and obliteration (Schneider 1990).

In these extremities we find the utmost consternations of humanity. Chaos is representative of unrelenting proliferation; it is the nightmare of mania, the end-state of ruthlessness and disarray. Obliteration, conversely, signifies never-ending collapse; it is the final outcome of isolation, the culmination of secrecy and disappearance.

Let me be clear that these are *unending* associations about which we are speaking, and the most powerful horror tales revel in them; mediocre horror tales, on the other hand, are not nearly so ambitious, nor are the classic mystery tales (à la Agatha Christie)—whereas the former evoke infinity, the latter settle for explicability.[2]

Although the infinity motif can be found in many other genres (e.g., romance and adventure stories), it is more *explicit* in the realms of horror. For example, romance novels refer to "boundless" passions, but it is doubtful that they intend the phrase literally; horror tales (à la *Frankenstein* and *Alien*) assuredly do. Adventure stories, similarly, flirt with the extraordinary (e.g., the island in *Swiss Family Robinson*), but rarely do they *dwell* in that dimension; the earthly, by contrast, is their preserve.

Although fairy tales can evoke the infinite (e.g., through witches, goblins, wizards, and the like), rarely are they equated with the horror genre. Science fiction can more frequently be grouped in the horror class (recall the sprawling bacterium in *The Andromeda Strain*), but here too we often find a distinction. This distinction centers on the expectations such stories create and the degree to which they fulfill those expectations. In his intriguing article on the "uncanny," Freud (1919/1958) elucidates this point:

> The uncanny . . . retains [its horrible] quality in fiction as in experience so long as the setting is one of physical reality; but as soon as it is given an arbitrary and unrealistic setting in fiction, it is apt to lose its quality of the uncanny. (p. 160)

The expectation generated by the story's setting, in other words, is pivotal. If the setting is unfathomable from the outset, as are most fairy tales and some works of science fiction, then the story is not likely to generate much horror. If, on the other hand, the setting is credible at its inception and *unexpectedly* becomes otherworldly, the story's shock-value mounts significantly. We are reminded once again of the role played by deviation: the more an experience deviates from and ultimately contradicts our accustomed outlook, the more intimidating it becomes. The characters in fairy stories are relatively easy to dismiss; they exist in "never-never" land. Monstrosities in horror classics, however, are disturbingly local; Hitchcock's *The Birds* is a case in point.

In short, horror is distinguished by two factors—the degree to which occurrences contradict expectations and the degree of extremity.

Freudian and Jungian Perspectives

Now let us consider the Freudian and Jungian explanations of horror, as these constitute the primary alternatives to our view.

Freud (1919/1958) classified "all that arouses . . . horror" as the "uncanny" (p. 122). After an exhaustive survey of possible definitions for this term, he arrives at one: "[it is] something familiar which has been repressed" (p. 155). This "familiarity," Freud contends, is "primitive"; it is a byproduct of "infantile complexes" (p. 157). These "complexes" include "animism, magic, . . . omnipotence of thoughts, . . . attitude[s] toward death, involuntary repetition, and . . . castration" fears, all of which are temporary "regressions," lapses in the "testing" of "reality" (pp. 143, 150, and 156).

The uncanny, then, is a fantastic regression. If I am aghast by a severed limb, childhood castration fears loom near. If spirits and ghosts appear to cross my path, early animistic beliefs can be blamed. If monstrosity is an issue, omnipotence fantasies can be ascribed, and so on.

Tribal beliefs are also viewed in this light. Witchcraft, incantation, demonism, immortal souls—all are products of arrested development (Freud, 1919/1958, pp. 147–48); all are echoes of that grandiose, paranoid state called infancy (p. 148).

Jung (1933), on the other hand, took issue with Freud's objectivism. Impressed by developments in modern physics (e.g., Heisenberg's Uncertainty Principle), Jung adopted a much broader view of reality. He implied that the uncanny exists regardless of age, culture, or social standing. The issue hinges on how it is interpreted. Westerners, Jung contends, provide rational explanations for the uncanny. For example, we attribute climatic disturbances to certain meteorological events. We explain sickness on a physiological basis. So-called primitives, on the other hand, explain these occurences on the basis of spirits and gods.

Who is more correct? Neither, according to Jung (1933). Both systems address aspects of the extraordinary, and both *work* for their respective cultures. In a later work, Jung (1961) suggests that what all cultures identify as uncanny is really just unassimilated psychic material. Our fears of darkness, sickness, the weather, and so on refer, at bottom, to our dread of consciousness in a cosmic sense, or of the Self archetype. This archetype, Jung implies, is benign in its totality (Jung 1961, p. 338). It is the all-encompassing unity of the psyche. Most of us dread the Self, however, because we can only assimilate small portions of it, leaving the balance to be borne by our religions.

While I have elsewhere set forth a more general critique of Jung and Freud (Schneider 1990), here I will confine myself very briefly to their views on horror. I find Freud's theory much too pat; horror, I believe, is neither primitive nor childish. Heisenberg's Uncertainty Principle aside, there are numerous instances of *realistic* horror in our lives. I agree with Jung here that the reality of the mind is inextricably bound up with the reality of the outside world and that *ultimate* reality is surely superordinate to reason.

I also question Freud's contention that horror is familiar. What is *familiar* about dematerialization, unstoppability, or cataclysm? While horror may include unintegrated aspects of one's past (for example, castration anxiety, magical thinking, intrauterine memories, and the like), these do not *demarcate* horror. As I have suggested, horror is demarcated not by specific content but by the *implications* of those contents. If horror was to begin and end with unassimilated sexual reminiscences, how much would there be to fret about? Once the reminiscences would be brought to awareness (i.e., assimilated), the horror would end. Indeed, this is what Freud implies. Mature people "surmount" it, he suggests (Freud, 1919/1958, p. 157).[3] But horror, like life, just does not work this way. By definition, horror cannot be surmounted. This is because horror implies *boundlessness*—the never-ending potentialities of the objects of our dread. Hence, it is not womb fantasies or castration complexes per se but the constrictive and expansive implications of those standpoints—their chaotic or obliterating possibilities—that concern us so.

While I find Jung to be refreshingly broadminded about horror, he too lapses into an all-too-consoling position. This is his belief (wish?) that the Self, like the radiant mandala which is purported to symbolize it, is harmonious.[4] Yet, as I have suggested, holism has no place in horror. To be sure, holism *may be* the underlying principle of consciousness, but the human capacity to doubt, to transcend innumerable forms of order and ideology, implies otherwise. This is the problem embodied in the question, "and what happens after that?" (meaning after one unites with the Self).

Accordingly, human beings probably cannot assimilate horror in any ultimate sense. We will always be skeptical of utopian remedies. This is because horror, as implied by infinity, does not "end" with childhood or historical archetypes but with space-time, and space-time *suspends,* it does not *ground.*

Before we turn to our analysis of the horror genre, let us summarize our position. The basis for horror is deviation, contradiction, and, ultimately, infinite constriction (obliteration) or expansion (chaos). While a glimpse of the polarities can be ecstatic, full disclosure is likely to be terrifying. The encounter with this terror, as opposed to its denial or passive acceptance, promotes vitality and social sensitivity.

Part II
Wisdom-Horror:
Dracula and *Frankenstein*

*Evil facts . . . may be the best key to
life's significance, and possibly the only
openers of our eyes to the deepest levels
of truth.*

—WILLIAM JAMES

Now let us consider our thesis from the standpoints of two
archetypal thrillers—Bram Stoker's *Dracula* (1897/1981) and
Mary Shelley's *Frankenstein* (1818/1981). I call these works
"archetypal" because of their great popularity and paradigmatic
plot structure. *Dracula,* for example, is a classic study in obliteration themes (hyperconstriction), *Frankenstein* a seminal inquiry
into the chaotic (hyperexpansion).

The degree to which these legends grip the imagination is
nothing short of phenomenal. Libraries overflow with their
influence. The movie industry never tires of their "spin-off"
potential. Our psyches burn with their seductive-repulsive implications. What could be more wondrous, many of us might ask,
than to be able to appear and disappear at will, to "mate" with an
immortal, or to "inspire" life into the dead? Alternatively, what
could be more trepidating?

As we consider the structure of these works, then, it is well to
bear in mind their power. Chaos and obliteration are as much
domains of the sacred as they are of the wretched (as previously
suggested), and *Dracula* and *Frankenstein* are richly versed in
both.[1] (Do not content yourself with my analysis only, however; I
strongly suggest that you steep yourself in the works first, then
consider my conclusions.)

Dracula and *Frankenstein,* finally, are not invariant models. *Dracula* highlights expansive themes *sometimes* and *Frankenstein,* constrictive; my concern here, however (as with each of the classics about to be presented), is with that which makes their respective brands of horror *unique.* The Dracula figure, for example, can certainly be understood as embodying some hyperexpansive elements. He has an insatiable appetite for blood, a wide range of mobility, and an enormous capacity to command. These traits, however (as I argue later), are not what put Dracula atop the pantheon of terrorizers: it is his forays into darkness and the microcosm, his cunning and stealthiness, that distinguish him. Frankenstein's monster, on the other hand, can assuredly flirt with hiddenness and the occult, but it is his physicality and riotous nature that differentiate him. Put simply, Dracula is to Frankenstein's monster what the snake is to the grizzly bear.

Beyond the *form* of their extremism, however, one point is clear: these behemoths of gothic lore both dwell in the outlands, the margins of our consciousness.

Bela Lugosi as Dracula. From *Dracula,* Universal, 1931. Copyright © by Universal City Studios, Inc. Courtesy of MCA Publishing Rights, a division of MCA Inc.

Dracula: A Study in Hyperconstriction

Dracula is a series of interrelated journal entries. Beginning with the records of Jonathan Harker, a British solicitor summoned by Count Dracula to help him purchase land in England, the journals wend their way through three related characters—Mina Murray, Harker's betrothed; Lucy Westenra, Mina's girlfriend; and Dr. Seward, Lucy's admirer and friend.

That hyperconstriction is *Dracula's* great thematic concern is hinted at early. Even before he sets out to meet the legendary figure, Harker notes: "Every known superstition in the world is gathered [in his land]"; it's "as if it were the centre of some sort of imaginative *whirlpool*" (p. 2, italics mine). Soon, Harker ventures forth to explore that whirlpool. After several train-rides, he arrives in Transylvania, at the foot of the Carpathian Mountains. As his carriage dashes into the mountains, he observes: "[it is] an endless perspective of jagged rock and pointed crags" (p. 7). The "falling sunset [throws] into strange relief the ghost-like clouds which amongst the Carpathians seem to wind ceaselessly through the valleys" (p. 8).

This imagery and foreshadowing is superb. We instantly identify with Harker. He is apprehensive, slowly feeling victimized by alien powers. He senses himself *sinking* into a gathering storm, a vortex that has no discernable base. Everything around him is darkening, "falling," and relentlessly encircling. Dracula, on the other hand, is the shadowy instigator of these forces. He is both revealed and concealed by them. We know that he is up to some evil, but all we are told early on is implied by "ghost-like clouds" and "jagged" rocks. We sense that Dracula is subtle, but all that is displayed in the early pages is a "ceaseless wind."

"There were dark, rolling clouds, . . . and in the air the

heavy, oppressive sense of thunder," Harker reports as he draws nearer to the castle (p. 9). Suddenly, a "hidden" driver with "coal-black" horses arrives to intercept Harker and conduct him on the last leg of his journey (p. 10). The riders of Harker's original carriage cross themselves, and he watches them ride off. "As they sank into the darkness," he tells us, "a strange chill, and a lonely feeling came over me" (p. 11).

"Soon we were hemmed in with trees," he continues, "which in places arched right over the roadway till we passed as through a tunnel; and again great frowning rocks guarded us" (p. 12). "The baying of . . . wolves," he goes on, "sounded nearer and nearer, as though they were closing round on us from every side" (p. 12). "[I felt a] paralysis of fear" (p. 13).

Finally, Harker's driver pulls up to "a vast ruined castle, from whose tall windows came no ray of light, and whose broken battlements showed a jagged line against the moonlit sky" (p. 14).

What can be seen here is that Harker is steeped in peril and gloom. He rides with a dark, faceless coachman. He is bounded by jet-black skies and "arching" trees, as if in a "tunnel." He is encircled by ravenous wolves. And he must now reside in a forbidding, broken-down castle.

At the same time, one cannot help but feel Harker's titillation over all this. There is something heady about journeying to a strange land. There is something brash about visiting a mysterious "dignitary." Harker is apprehensive, but he is also daring and curious about the meaning of his dilemmas. The imagery of concealment—dark skies, clouds, tunnels, the anonymous coachman—are tinged with excitement as well as trepidation. We wonder what secrets they hold. What powers are contained within them? The imagery of entrapment—feeling hemmed in, surrounded, hunted—likewise can also elate. They can suggest closeness, containment, and intimacy, as well as oppression. The sense of sinking, similarly, suggests the wish to "let go," to be "swallowed up" by a power greater than oneself, to Be in a cosmic sense. We shall note many similar associations momentarily.

The second chapter of *Dracula* reinforces our consternation. His castle is a dark, obscure place, Harker informs us. "Several dark ways led from it under great round arches" (p. 15).

Harker "could not but notice" the coachman's hand—"like a steel vice that could have crushed" his own hand (p. 15). As the coachman and carriage departed, they "disappeared down one of the dark openings" (p. 15).

Harker stands "in silence" (p. 15). He feels as if the castle's "frowning walls and dark window openings" cannot be "penetrate[d]" (p. 15). "Doubts and fears" crowd upon him as he waits for the Count to greet him (p. 15).

At this point the reader might protest: "but what *specifically* do these descriptions have to do with hyperconstriction (obliteration)? They can just as easily, and perhaps more logically, be explained on Freudian grounds." For example, Harker's references to "dark openings," being "crushed," and "penetrating" are classical womb-associations.

While this reservation has face validity, it is not entirely faithful to the phenomenon under study. Harker's terror—and hence our own—cannot be reduced to specific contents. It is not to be found in the parts of a person's anatomy. It is to be found in the mood set by those objects—their *spatio-temporal* connotations. "Dark openings," for example, may tell us about Harker's fear of the womb, but it also conjures up his dread of the unknown, the fathomless, and the unending. His concern with being crushed relates to an intrauterine experience, perhaps, but it also conveys his sense of diminishment and utter powerlessness. Finally, his inability to penetrate the castle walls further underscores his plight. We will understand more about these dynamics as we proceed.

Harker's sense of being "closed in," of *sinking*, was hardly assuaged by Dracula's appearance. A "tall" man, clad completely in "black," Dracula could not be more sardonic: "Welcome to my house! Enter freely and of your own will!" (p. 16).

A short time later, however, the count was more direct: "You may go anywhere you wish in the castle, except where the doors are locked, where of course you will not wish to go" (p. 21). Suddenly, we are perturbed. What is behind the locked doors? What secrets are concealed? In time we learn that the castle is very old. This, in fact, is what Dracula likes about the English house that Harker describes to him. Dracula, we learn, derives from an ancient, warlike clan. He and his fortress are witnesses to many battles, the spilling of much blood. There are numerous mysteries associated with this legacy, not the least of which is Dracula's fondness for the night. "I love the shade and shadow," he tells us, "and would be alone with my thoughts when I may" (p. 24).

Chapter Three opens with a very uncomfortable realization: Harker is a "prisoner" (p. 29). While we receive some preparation for this condition from the outset, it is still quite jarring. More than ever, Harker is convinced of his helplessness. He peers out his window and sees dark, "narrow courtyards" (p. 34). Inaccessible as they are, however, there is some "sense of freedom" in the surrounding "expanse" (p. 34). He gazes down the castle walls as if into an "abyss" (p. 35). He sees Dracula "crawl down" those very same walls and "vanish into some hole" (p. 36). He searches vainly for an unlocked door or portal of escape. He is "encompassed about" by "terrors" (p. 35).

And then it happens. His worst fear, his most dreaded nightmare, comes to pass. After a long day of searching for ways to escape, he settles into a half-slumber on an old musty couch. This is in the "ladies" section of the castle, he writes, where maidens of old resided. Suddenly, three young women are opposite him. They have "brilliant white teeth" and "voluptuous lips" (pp. 37–38). One of them reminds him of some "dreamy fear" (p. 38). "There was something about them," he conveys, that makes him "desire that they would kiss [him] with those red lips" (p. 39). And yet he is deathly afraid of them as well (p. 39). One girl advances toward him. Her breath is "honey sweet" and yet "underlying" is a bitterness that "one smells in blood" (p. 39). "There was a deliberate voluptuousness," he tells us, "both thrilling and repulsive" (p. 39). He could feel her "hot breath on [his] neck" (p. 39). He "closed his eyes in a languorous ecstasy and waited—waited with beating heart" for her touch (p. 39).

But instantly he is awakened by another presence. It is the Count whisking the women away! He could see "fury" in the Count's eyes and "blazing . . . passion" in his cheeks (p. 40). He watched anxiously as one of the women let out a "low wail" (p. 40). With great haste, the Count pulled them all away, and as "shadowy forms," they faded into the night (p. 41). A "horror" overcame Harker, as he "sank . . . into unconsciousness" (p. 41).

In time, Harker awakens from this semi-conscious dread. Half-dazed, and infuriated, he searches wildly about the house to subdue the monster. Finally, he discovers Dracula's daytime secret. He replenishes his fiendish energies by sealing himself up in a coffin. Hastily, Harker pries open the "great box," grabs a nearby shovel, and attempts to pummel the Count. These *human* efforts, however, prove futile. One searing glance from the Count and Harker is "paralysed" (p. 54). His shovel—and plans—are aborted. Devil "of the pit!" (p. 55), Harker exclaims.

Before we consider our tale further, it is useful to summarize our findings, which are really the axes upon which the balance of the story revolves. The essential concern of these opening chapters is concealment, surrender, and ultimately obliteration. Dracula is a tricky, obscure figure who spends most of his time in darkness. Those who accompany him are also shadowy and thrive, as he does, on "hidden" matters. These include not only physical dimensions, such as coffins and blood, but emotions as well. They prey upon Harker's innocence, for example, exploiting both his dreams and professional skills.

Surrender is highlighted by Harker's submission to—and occassional fascination with—the Count. From the outset Harker loses strength ("sinks"), grows isolated ("lonely," "chilled"), and becomes trapped ("encircled by doom," "hemmed in by wolves"). He feels increasingly victimized ("hypnotized," entranced, dominated) by the Count and his "assistants." He grows dependent on them, feels he has no choice but to accept what they present to him, and becomes despondent.

The pattern that emerges here is of one of initial fascination but eventual (or abrupt) despair. The more that Harker encounters contradictions the greater is his dismay. For example, Harker is intrigued, even excited, by the ghostly women, but he is petrified by the dark, parasitic world in which they dwell. Likewise, he is awed by Dracula's cleverness, but he is bowled over by its potential for harm.

The crux of Harker's trepidation, then, is the implication of these dilemmas. The final destination of concealment and surrender is obliteration, whether of objects or of power. What other conclusion can we or Harker arrive at? Harker's world is diminishing, and he is alarmed by the proportions.

Harker's fiancée, Mina, leads off the next section of *Dracula.* Mina's entry is a letter to her close friend Lucy, detailing Harker's latest note to her. He is "well" she conveys, hoping to be home in "a week" (pp. 57–58). (Dracula, of course, forced Harker to communicate such reassuring news.)

Mina then inquires as to Lucy's relationship with her fiancée, Arthur Holmwood. Lucy responds in a letter indicating that she and Mr. Holmwood are fine but that another intriguing man, Dr. Jonathan Seward, has entered her life. It seems that Holmwood introduced Seward, who at the age of twenty-nine runs a "lunatic asylum" (p. 58). Seward is apparently quite taken with Lucy. Lucy is flattered but does not reject Holmwood.

Several pages later, we are presented with Dr. Seward's diary. He conveys that a particular asylum inmate, Renfield, has occupied his interest of late. Seward indicates that Renfield is collecting and consuming flies, writing meticulous lists, and being "generally selfish, secretive, and purposeful." "Oh unconscious cerebration!" Seward exclaims (p. 73). There must be "method in his madness" (p. 73).

Meantime, Mina Harker is becoming increasingly concerned about her betrothed Jonathan and her good friend Lucy. She has not heard from Jonathan for several months, and Lucy, who is visiting Mina, is engaging in eerie behavior. For example, Mina reports that Lucy is sleepwalking frequently and wanders about outdoors. Mina describes this environment as misty and vast. "The clouds are piled up like giant rocks, and there is a 'brool' over the sea that sounds like some presage of doom. Dark figures are on the beach," she goes on, "half shrouded in the mist" (p. 77).

Mina's anticipation of doom is soon vindicated as a great storm blows through the area. "Then came another rush of sea-fog . . . a mass of dank mist, which seemed to close on all things . . ." (p. 83). "Billows" of thunder "came through the damp oblivion . . ." (p. 83).

Suddenly a strange shape is spotted on the horizon. It is a ship, which had been mysteriously abandoned. A reporter investigating the story (whom Mina quotes) finds the captain's log and relates that there was "some doom over this ship" (p. 88). Later he reports that "there was a strange man aboard" who terrorized the ship. He quotes one of the crewmen: " 'On the watch last night I saw It, like a man, tall and thin, and ghastly pale . . . I crept behind It, and gave It my knife, but the knife went through It empty as air' " (p. 90).

Mina Harker meanwhile is getting increasingly worried about Lucy. She went after Lucy one night—"the time and distance seemed endless"—and found her "reclining with her head lying over the back of" a churchyard bench (p. 96). Lucy's "lips were parted, and she was breathing . . . in long, heavy gasps, as though striving to get her lungs full at every breath" (p. 97). Additionally, her "throat was pierced" by "two . . . pin-pricks" (p. 98).

Step by step, now, our tale begins to cohere. Dr. Seward is summoned by Holmwood to examine Lucy, and Mina hears from Jonathan, who is convalescing at a Budapest hospital. Jonathan is emotionally paralyzed. Lucy is spellbound. Seward tries magnanimously to understand Lucy but cannot. He does, however, sense that there is more at work here than ordinary disease. Mina has that feeling about Jonathan as well. It is at this point that Dr. Abraham Van Helsing is contacted, at Seward's behest. Van Helsing, who is Seward's mentor, is Dracula's alter ego. He is the only man that Seward knows who is as fascinated as he is terrified by occult phenomena, and he has had many dealings in this area. Van Helsing, Seward expounds, is "a philosopher and . . . metaphysician, and one of the most advanced scientists of his day" (p. 119).

The stage is now set for our novel's central conflict—that between the fascination with and terror of the infinitesimal. Most of *Dracula's* characters are intimidated by the deepening dilemmas. Jonathan is exhausted and bedridden; Mina is apprehensive and confused; Lucy is victimized; Holmwood is helpless; and Seward is intrigued but is in quite "over his head." Only Van Helsing, the heroically "open-minded" investigator can match wits with Dracula (p. 119); only Van Helsing can energetically venture into hidden realms.

Let us consider this prospect further. In order to deal with Dracula you need someone who can penetrate his world. You need someone who can pursue its depths so as to unbalance and subdue him. You also need someone who knows his own limits—the limits of the human being—so as to avoid unproductive action, false hope, and self-destruction. In short, you need someone both clever and brave, thorough yet creative—someone *integrated.*

Van Helsing, then, is the embodiment of this adventurer-type. He will discover, to the point possible, Dracula's aims and methods, and he will use them against Dracula so that he can be stopped.

Seward can thus say about Van Helsing:

> He has an absolutely open mind. This with an iron nerve, a temper of the ice-brook, an indomitable resolution, self-command, and toleration exalted from virtues to blessings, and the kindliest and truest heart that beats—these form his equipment for the noble work that he is doing for mankind . . . for his views are as wide as his all-embracing sympathy. (p. 119).

The pall of Dracula, meanwhile, is increasingly manifest. Steadily, his mark is being felt. Subtly, and sometimes explosively, he creeps into the lives of our protagonists, prompting the curiosity of some, wearing down the energy of others. Lucy's condition worsens. She is pale and chronically bedridden. She is given many blood transfusions, but she invariably reverts to her former state. At Van Helsing's request, garlic is strewn about the room, but it is removed by Lucy's unwary mother. Lucy is terrified to sleep: sleep holds "unknown horrors" for her (p. 140).

Suddenly, Lucy experiences a temporary reprieve. She writes:

> I have a dim half-remembrance of long, anxious times of waiting and fearing; darkness in which there was not even the pain of hope . . . ; and then long spells of oblivion, and the rising back to life as a diver coming up through a great press of water. (p. 143)

But Lucy's optimism fades as quickly as it arrives. A haunting force continues to beckon her. Bat-shapes are visible at her window. Their flapping wings and the howl of wolves in the distance can be detected. "The air seems full of specks," she writes of a particularly disturbing night, "floating and encircling in the [draft] from the window, and the lights burn blue and dim" (p. 152).

"A terrible fear" begins "to assail" Seward, meanwhile, as he contemplates the "chain of doom which seemed drawing tight around" them (p. 153).

In time, Arthur Holmwood arrives to assist Drs. Seward and Van Helsing with Lucy. Mina and Jonathan Harker also return from their ordeal. Mina records Jonathan's delirious yet detailed account of his visit with the Count, which delights Van Helsing: "This paper is sunshine," he quips, because it throws significant light on Dracula's aims and methods (p. 193).

Reports of a "bloofer [or ghost] lady," meantime, are on the rise. Several children have reportedly been abducted by this lady and have been wounded in the throat. In contrast to the others, Van Helsing understands the implications of these tragedies. He understands that Lucy has now fallen totally under Dracula's spell.

In order to persuade the others that he is right, Van Helsing waxes eloquent:

> 'Ah, it is the fault of our science that it wants to explain all; and if it explain not, then it says there is nothing to explain. . . . I suppose now you do not believe in corporeal transference. No? Nor in materialisation? . . . Nor in astral bodies . . . Nor in the reading of thought . . . Nor in hypnotism—' (pp. 200– 201)

Seward retorts that Charcot "has proved [hypnotism] pretty well" (p. 201). Van Helsing then challenges Seward to entertain even stranger phenomena:

> Then tell me—for I am a student of the brain—how you accept hypnotism and reject thought reading. Let me tell you, my friend, that there are things done to-day in electrical science which would have been deemed unholy by the very men who discovered electricity—who would themselves not so long before have been burned as wizards. (p. 201)

"There are always mysteries in life," concludes Van Helsing (p. 201). With this resounding declaration, Van Helsing prepares the group for his next ghastly revelation: Lucy "made the small holes in the children's throats" (p. 203)!

What we are shown here then is that Van Helsing is Dracula's double. Both he and Dracula draw from the realms of the occult, but that which Dracula uses to promote destruction, Van Helsing employs to foster health. Second, Van Helsing, in his wisdom, acknowledges the limits of science. Though it can go very far—in this case into the microcosm—there are always further puzzles. Dracula, on the other hand, transcends science. He is a metaphor for the occult. He represents all that stirs among quanta and microbes—thought-reading, materialization, corporeal transference, astral bodies.

Dracula, Van Helsing elaborates,

> is of cunning more than mortal, for his cunning be the growth of ages . . . all the dead that he can come nigh to are for him at command; he is brute, and more than brute; he is devil in callous, and the heart of him is not; he can, within limitations, appear at will when, and where, and in any of the forms that are to him; he can, within his range, direct the elements; the storm, the fog, the thunder; he can command all the meaner things: the rat, and the owl, and the bat—the moth, and the fox, and the wolf: he can grow and become small; and he can at times vanish and come unknown. (p. 250)

Elsewhere, Van Helsing states that Dracula

> can come in mist which he create[s]—that noble ship's captain proved him of this. . . . He [can] come on moonlight rays as elemental dust—as . . . Jonathan [Harker] saw . . . in the castle of Dracula. He [can] become so small— . . . slip[ping] through a hairbreadth space. . . . He can, when once he find his way, come out from anything or into anything, no matter how close it be bound or even fused up with fire. . . . He can see in the dark . . . (p. 253)

Despite these supernatural powers, however, Dracula *is not* omnipotent. He is *limited,* as Van Helsing indicates. By day, for example, he is confined to a coffin and vulnerable to eradication. By night, he is stymied by the cross, garlic cloves, and holy wafers. He can only appear and disappear at *certain* places and times. Even "he who is not nature," Van Helsing observes, "has yet to obey some of nature's laws—" (p. 253). "Why we know not," Van Helsing muses (p. 253).

Hence, our excursion into the infinitesimal embraces three tiers. The first level is that of science, with its rational laws and discoveries. The second level is that of Dracula, with his abundant knowledge of the occult; Van Helsing too has assimilated some of this knowledge. The third level, finally, is that of Being (or God or the holy), with its *limitlessness.*

Yet because Van Helsing grasps portions of Dracula's world, he begins to unveil the keys to his demise. He realizes that to subdue Dracula, the protagonists must think like him and use his methods. Van Helsing thus instructs the group in occult interventions. He leads them to Lucy, who is by now one of Dracula's "undead" servants. The protagonists' horrible task is to open her crypt and drive a stake through her heart. Next, they must pursue Dracula himself, who holds their lives and those of countless others in the balance.

The essence of Van Helsing's plan is to enter Dracula's English home (specifically, the chapel nearby), locate and pry open the "unholy" caskets, and "sterilize" them (p. 315). This is done by placing "holy" wafers in the dirt which Dracula packed around the corpses. Van Helsing elaborates:

> And now, my friends, we have a duty here to do. We must sterilize this earth, so sacred of holy memories, that he has brought from a far distant land for such fell use. He has chosen this earth because it has been holy. Thus we defeat him with his own weapon, for we make it more holy still. It was sanctified to such use of man, now we sanctify it to God. (p. 315)

Upon the completion of this work, Van Helsing convinces the group to pursue Dracula, who has by this time begun a retreat to his native land. The group, however, has not totally escaped Dracula's influence. Just earlier, he unleashed his bloodlust upon Mina and began the process of hypnotically controlling her. Mina, in fact, was Dracula's "trump card," as he would use her to lure the others into his trap.

"I felt my strength fading away," Mina recalls of the incident, "and I was in a half-swoon. How long this horrible thing lasted I

27

know not; but it seemed that a long time must have passed before he took his foul, awful, sneering mouth away" (p. 304). Seward, the recorder of these observations, comments: "The remembrance seemed for awhile to *overpower* her, and she *drooped* and would have *sunk down* but for her husband's sustaining arm" (p. 304, italics mine).

Mina recalls further that Dracula admonished her and the others for playing their "brains against" his and frustrating him in his "designs" (p. 304). "You know now . . . what it is to cross my path," he barked (p. 304). "God pity me!"—Mina cries to her associates. "Look down on a poor soul in worse than mortal peril!"

Despite Mina's growing sense of being engulfed, Van Helsing holds firm. He pleads with her: "You must struggle and strive to live, though death would seem a boon unspeakable. You must fight Death himself, though he come to you in pain or in joy; by the day, or the night; in safety or in peril!" (p. 308). Mina promises to do her best, but the struggle is great.

Van Helsing plots the steps ahead. He knows that Dracula periodically contacts Mina to increase his control over her and compel her to do his bidding. Van Helsing, however, turns this strategy against the Count, by hypnotizing Mina and entreating her to reveal information about *his* movements. This strategy proves successful at first and helps the group close in on Dracula. But as Mina fades in and out of her trance, and never quite establishes her allegiance, the group starts to tire. Dracula "is growing," Van Helsing warns (p. 320). "He is experimenting, and doing it well; and if it had not been that we . . . crossed his path he would be yet—he may be yet if we fail—the . . . furtherer of a new order of beings, whose road must lead through death, not life" (p. 320).

He is "creeping into knowledge experimentally," Van Helsing goes on (p. 320). He "has been making use of" hypnosis and the divination of the dead to spread his influence (p. 320). If "he had dared, at the first, to attempt certain things, he would long ago have been beyond our power" (p. 320).

Step by step, however, the group moves closer to Dracula's lair. Finally, they enter his country. It is a startling terrain, brimming with subtleties and torments. "The very place," Van Helsing marvels, where [Dracula has] been alive, Un-dead for all these centuries, is full of strangeness of the geologic and chemical world. There are deep caverns and fissures that reach none know whither. There have been volcanoes, some of whose openings still send out waters of strange properties, and gases that kill or make to vivify. Doubtless, there is something magnetic or electric in some of these combinations of occult forces which work for physical life in strange way; and in himself were from the first some great qualities. (p. 338)

Mina, meanwhile, lapses in and out of Dracula's control. Sunrise and sunset "are to her times of peculiar freedom; when her old self can be manifest without any controlling force subduing and restraining her, or inciting her to action" (p. 348).

Despite her deterioration, however, Mina is determined to help the group (which now includes two more friends, Lord Godalming and Quincey Morris) to eradicate the Count. She knows that the others could drive a stake through her heart (as with Lucy) and provide her with "eternal rest," but she does not choose this option (p. 349). Instead, she perseveres into "the blackest things that the world or nether-world holds" (p. 349).

Bolstered by telepathic insight, Mina guides the men to Dracula's hideout. It is a carriage, protected by gypsies. The group overtakes the gypsies, pry open Dracula's "box," and plunge their knives into his "pale" corpse (p. 398). Instantly, Mina tells us, the "body crumbled into dust and passed from our sight" (p. 398).

Dracula is a study of one side of infinity or the holy. It is a dizzying journey into concealment, seduction, and obliteration. At first we are captivated, even enchanted, by these conditions. Harker, for example, is stunned by the "beauty" of Dracula's terrain and finds its legends "interesting." Yet the deeper Harker probes, the greater is his dismay. Dracula's terrain is *too* exotic. His powers are *excessively* subtle.

Dr. Seward is also initially intrigued by Dracula. He is a fascinating specimen, a scientific phenomenon, for Seward. This "glow," however, is temporary. As soon as Seward grasps the occult nature of Dracula's activity, he is stunned. The "glow" quickly fades. Empirical knowledge (i.e., that which can be perceived through the five senses), Seward realizes, is impotent in the face of the Count's telepathic, hypnotic, and telekinetic powers.

Only Van Helsing is wise enough to pursue Dracula in his fullness. From the outset, he is "realistic" about Dracula. Van Helsing acknowledges Dracula's ability to seduce, but he does not forget the Count's equally profound destructiveness. He observes Dracula's genius for subatomic manipulations, but he never discounts the unsettling consequences of these manipulations. He is a lover of science and religion, but he bristles at the arrogance of his associates. He contends that "true" science and religion approach the world in exploratory rather than absolutist terms and that the only way to address elusive phenomena (such as Dracula) is *both* by keeping an open mind *and* in knowing one's limitations. For example, the protagonists would not have understood Dracula's methods, had they not consulted "supernatural" sources (arcane books, experts on the occult, etc.); they would not have been able to slay Dracula had they attempted to physically overpower him or use extant scientific procedures. These were superfluous, Van Helsing cautioned.

Despite Dracula's eventual destruction, Van Helsing (whom we can presume is Stoker's philosophical "voice") leaves us with few comforts. What, for example, does he imply when he states that "There are always mysteries" or that even Dracula has his "limits"? He implies, I believe, that *Dracula* is not simply about a monster, it is about the mysterious force which permits monstrosities. It is about a "God" who can be both angelic and devilish, ally and antagonist (see Otto 1958).

Dracula was defeated, Van Helsing suggests, precisely because that which enabled him now dispels him. Just as in the story of Job, the central question of *Dracula* is, "who and what is God, and how does one cope bereft of this knowledge?" Although we are given no clear answers to this query (à la *Job*), Van Helsing does provide some stimulating directions. He suggests that, at bottom, divinity is a "void," to use Tillich's phrase, an infinite-infinitesimal power. Although we must struggle to harness this power, we must always be wary of its capacity to overwhelm. We must resist both dogmatic inferences concerning it and false hopes; by contrast, we must walk humbly before it and continually prepare for its challenges.

Boris Karloff as Frankenstein's Monster. From *Frankenstein,* Universal, 1931. Copyright © by Universal City Studios, Inc. Courtesy of MCA Publishing Rights, a division of MCA Inc.

Frankenstein: A Study in Hyperexpansion

Frankenstein is a tale about unchecked zeal. It is a window on human greed and presumption. What happens, the novel inquires, when we mobilize the grandest forces of nature, when we achieve the boldest feats of technology? What happens when we flirt with God-like powers? If *Dracula* is a study in the subtle and occult side of consciousness, *Frankenstein* is an exploration of the overt and grotesque aspects of consciousness. It is an inquiry into passion, power, and eventual chaos.

Frankenstein opens with radiant anticipation. Robert Walton, a sea-faring adventurer, sets out from London for the North Pole. His aim is to discover the causes of gravitation and planetary movements. At the North Pole he envisions: "The sun is forever visible, its broad disk just skirting the horizon and diffusing a perpetual splendour" (p. 1). "I may discover," he goes on, "the wondrous power which attracts the needle and may regulate a thousand celestial observations" (pp. 1–2).

Instantly, we are drawn to the excitement of this opening. Here is a man charged with passion, eager to explore. It does not matter to Walton that he will be far from civilization or that his journey is racked with perils. The immensity of his undertaking is of no consequence. He is afire, dazzled by the universe. "I feel my heart glow with an enthusiasm which elevates me to heaven," he writes to his sister (p. 2).

But Walton's exuberance wanes. "I have no friend," he laments (p. 5).

> It is true that I have thought more and that my daydreams are more extended and magnificent [than others'], but I greatly

need a friend who would have sense enough not to despise me as romantic, and affection enough . . . to endeavor to regulate my mind. (p. 5).

As Walton nears his destination his excitement resurges. He writes to his sister: "I cannot describe to you my sensation on the near prospect of my undertaking" (p. 7). He compares his "attachment to . . . the dangerous mysteries of ocean," to that "production of the most imaginative poets" (p. 7). "There is something at work in my soul," he goes on

> which I do not understand. I am practically industrious— painstaking, a workman to execute with perseverence and labour, but besides this there is a love for the marvellous, a belief in the marvellous, intertwined in all my projects, which hurries me out of the common pathways of men, even to the wild sea and unvisited regions I am about to explore. (p. 7)

Walton's descriptions form an exquisite backdrop to the events ahead, as we shall see.

Presently, Walton spots a "gigantic" figure dashing across the ice caps (p. 9). Although he is puzzled by the entity, he is unable to pursue it. A day later, Walton's crew spots another sledge which has drifted toward their ship. The driver, a weary European, is helped on board and introduced to Walton (who is also the ship's captain). The sickly traveler is instantly appealing to Walton: "I never saw a more interesting creature," he exclaims (p. 11). "His eyes have generally an expression of wildness, and even madness" (p. 11). This attraction is reciprocated and so begins the unfolding of our tale.

The traveler is Dr. Victor Frankenstein, and his story not only parallels but unsparingly magnifies Walton's. Frankenstein, in fact, is a mentor of sorts, endeavoring to alert Walton to myriad dangers. "You seek for knowledge and wisdom," Frankenstein warns, "and I ardently hope that the gratification of your wishes may not be a serpent to sting you, as mine has been" (p. 15). He continues:

> I do not know that the relation of my disasters will be useful to you; yet when I reflect that you are pursuing the same course, exposing yourself to the same dangers which have rendered me

> what I am, I imagine that you may deduce an apt moral from
> my tale, one that may direct you if you succeed in your
> undertaking and console you in case of failure. (p. 15)

Frankenstein goes on to divulge his life-story to Walton. He emerged from the "happiest" childhood, he gushes (p. 23). His parents were caring and generous. His adopted sister Elizabeth became his "beautiful and adored companion" (p. 21). The devotion and support heaped upon him as a youth gave him ample room to exercise his talents. His parents' struggles gave him the impetus to transcend even their resilience and resourcefulness.

The desire to learn about the physical world, however, was young Frankenstein's chief obsession. "It was the secrets of heaven and earth that I desired to learn," he relates to Walton (p. 23).

> And whether it was the outward substance of things or the
> mysterious soul of man that occupied me, still my inquiries
> were directed to the metaphysical, or in it[s] highest sense, the
> physical secrets of the world. (p. 23)

This preoccupation with physical and cosmic power is one of the hallmarks of Mary Shelley's novel. (Witness, for example, its numerous references to vastness and quantity.) As we shall see, *Frankenstein* is a highly *sensate* work.

Continuing with his recollections, Frankenstein tells Walton about the other important figure in his life, his kind, dedicated friend, Henry Clerval. If Frankenstein was entranced by the physical world, Clerval was concerned with the "moral" and virtuous, although this, unfortunately, had little affect on Frankenstein's own philosophical musings (p. 23).

The years passed, and Frankenstein's passion for learning and knowledge "swelled" (p. 24). "It became the torrent which, in its course, . . . swept away all [his] hopes and joys" (p. 24). As he became more sophisticated, Frankenstein indulged in "Natural Philosophy" (the forerunner of natural science) (p. 24). He wanted to do something great, perhaps in cosmology, perhaps in medicine. He read ancient metaphysical tracts. He saw that philosophers knew little more than "peasants" about the "mystery" of nature, and endeavored desperately to alter this condition (p. 25). His central desire soon began to take shape: he wanted to "banish disease from the human frame and render man invulnerable to any but a violent death" (p. 26). But this vision waned for long periods, as the youthful scientist "floundered" in a "slough of multifarious knowledge" (p. 26).

In time, Frankenstein began formal studies. Fascinated by lightning, electricity, and chemistry, he plunged into scholarship. Although he admired the "grandeur" of the ancient thinkers, he lamented their crude techniques. And while he admired the science of his day, he decried its philosophical narrowness. Soon, however, Frankenstein encountered a charismatic professor who helped him to reconcile his conflict. Modern science, this professor suggested, can do much more than perform mundane tasks. It "has new and almost unlimited powers; [it] can command the thunders of heaven, mimic the earthquake, and even mock the invisible world with its own shadows" (p. 33). Words like these inspired Frankenstein and deepened his self-confidence (if not grandiosity):

> So much has been done, . . . more, far more, will I achieve; treading in the steps already marked, I will pioneer a new way, explore unknown powers, and unfold to the world the deepest mysteries of creation (p. 33).

"I closed my eyes that night," Frankenstein relates to Walton (p. 33). "My internal being was in a state of insurrection and turmoil" (p. 33).

Let us pause at this point and reflect upon Frankenstein's state of exaltation. He speaks of "immortality and power," "boundless grandeur," "insurrection and turmoil," and "ardour" (pp. 32–35). Even more than Walton, he is intoxicated with ambition. Yet Frankenstein's passion is not merely *self*-aggrandizing. To be sure, he *is* self-absorbed, but his vision embraces more than himself. It encompasses the hopes and dreams of humanity. At least this is how I interpret his scientific curiosity and desire to extend life.

At the same time, there is something disturbing about Frankenstein's zeal. We begin to wonder if he has control over his project; or if it is too vast and unpredictable? Walton has already admitted as much about his own aspirations, which need to be "regulated" from time to time.

Continuing with his tale, Frankenstein recollects his growing interest in physiology and particularly in the extension of life. He applied a "supernatural enthusiasm" to this area, working day and night (p. 36). He became "dizzy with the immensity" of his undertaking (p. 37). Finally, like a bolt from the blue, came his discovery of how to animate "lifeless matter" (p. 37).

In time, Frankenstein decided to apply himself to the supreme endeavor—creation of a human being. Hence, from scraps of dead bodies, Frankenstein undertook to erect a great and powerful being who could perhaps spawn a similar race of beings. This conception was like a "hurricane" that Frankenstein began with "breathless eagerness" and "unremitting ardor" (pp. 38–39).

Again, however, Frankenstein is self-critical with Walton: "Learn from me . . . how dangerous is the acquirement of knowledge . . . [for him] who aspires to become greater than his nature will allow" (p. 38).

Here we have it, then, the essence of the narrative. Zeal is elevating, ideas are ennobling; but how expansive can people be? Do we not err in even the most remarkable works of art and science? Can we genuinely foresee the implications of our work? Instantly, for example, Frankenstein is in a bind. How will he get body parts for his creation—steal them from laboratories, dig up graves? Can he tolerate these transgressions? Can he face the horrors of transplants and decay? And what of our *contemporary* "Frankenstein's monsters"—the splitting of the atom, genetic engineering, mass transit, industrial waste, high technology? Where will these lead, as they spread across our mental and physical terrains?

I am reminded here of some of the "manic" clients I have encountered. These people couldn't slow down, couldn't get perspective on their capacities, couldn't channel their energies and be self-critical. Their speech was extraordinarily rapid, their cravings for pleasure and excitement were unworldly. They became so filled with ideas, dreams, and desires that no one— not even close friends—could alert them to the danger ahead, the inevitable "crash" that befalls any overloaded organism or system. Such is the case with Frankenstein's aspirations.

What began as adventurous and hopeful for Frankenstein, now turns disconcerting. "My enthusiasm was checked by my anxiety," he tells Walton (p. 41).

As his work progressed, Frankenstein encountered further uncertainties. His creation could not, for practical reasons, appear normal; it became "gigantic." The skin, of necessity, turned "yellow." The monster became so hideous in fact that "no mortal could support the horror of [its] countenance" (p. 43).

Despite his exuberance, Frankenstein too grew increasingly repulsed by his creature. As he watched it writhe and stir to life, he became sick with regret. Finally, he too reached the point of intolerance for the entity and summarily abandoned it.

The balance of the story is well-known. The monster ventures forth into the world on its own. It experiences numerous degradations and rejections. The foremost "blow" occurs in a small cottage in the forest. The creature had been observing this cottage for months, yearning to meet its inhabitants. These people struck the creature as the quintessence of generosity and fore-bearance. At the crucial moment of encountering the family, however, the creature is severely reproved. This enrages the creature and it departs: "When night came," the creature tells us,

> I quitted my retreat and wandered in the wood; and now, no longer restrained by the fear of discovery, I gave vent to my anguish in fearful howlings. I was like a wild beast that had broken the toils, destroying the objects that obstructed me and ranging through the wood with a stag-like swiftness.
>
> "I . . . bore a hell within me," the creature elaborates, and finding myself unsympathized with, wished to tear up the trees, spread havoc and destruction around me . . . From that moment I declared everlasting war against the species, and more than all, against him who had formed me and sent me forth to this unsupportable misery. (p. 121)

The creature, accordingly, turns its fury toward Frankenstein. What began as a dream, as a grand humanitarian project, is now an unbridled destroyer. That which was engineered for swiftness, strength, and resiliency is transformed into a vengeful, contemptuous "wretch" (p. 170). All the qualities, which when controlled promote social welfare, now promote havoc.

The creature permits Frankenstein one last chance to "redeem" himself. "Create for me a female companion," he, in effect, bellows. Frankenstein rejects this demand also, however, and the monster vows that "not only you and your family but thousands of others, shall be swallowed up in the whirlwinds of [my] rage" (p. 84).

Reflecting on *Frankenstein* in terms of our thesis, several points become evident. First, ecstasy follows the same trajectory as that in *Dracula,* with one exception: whereas the characters in *Dracula* are initially intrigued by *constrictive* themes (surrender, concealment); those in *Frankenstein* are captivated by *expansive* motifs (cosmology, life-extension, physical power). Walton, for example, traverses perilous seas to investigate gravity and planetary motion. Frankenstein endures even greater hardships to harness the forces of life. These exaltations, however, (just as those in *Dracula*) give way to wariness, wariness to dread, and dread to horror. Let us look more closely at the development of this sequence.

Exaltation is a state of well-being. It is based on a sense of social or cosmic comfort. The exalted person feels (even if only vaguely) that "all is well with the world" and that no matter what happens—self-annihilation notwithstanding—everything "is as it should be." People, life, the cosmos, are *contained, supported.*

This state of consciousness, however, is illusory for both Stoker and Shelley. For example, Harker is enchanted by the Carpathian Mountains only within the context of a safe, orderly journey. He is intrigued by Dracula's eccentricities only to the degree that they have a culturally recognizable context, such as wealth or royalty. Walton, likewise, marvels at the earth's geological forces but chiefly within the purview of natural science. Frankenstein is dazzled at the prospect of cultivating human life, but only so long as it is a *manageable* enterprise. In short, exaltation is both a structured and temporary condition.

Yet "every angel is terrifying," as Rilke (1982, p. 151) intimates, and the further our characters venture into uncharted terrain, the greater is their bewilderment. We have already explored the outcome of this bewilderment in *Dracula;* now let us consider its unfoldment in *Frankenstein.* Frankenstein's confrontation with the "horrible" begins with the construction of his being. Here, he is faced with exhumation and the morbid assemblage of body parts. The sight before him is so ugly, so foreign, that he can barely tolerate "its countenance." With brutal suddenness, he is confronted with the enormity of his undertaking. Doubts begin to creep in. He asks in effect, "What am I really attempting to do? Can I control the consequences of this project?"

As time progresses, Frankenstein's creature becomes even more gruesome and unpredictable. It grovels for food and shelter. It flounders about in physical and psychological confusion. It fumbles through the world encountering disappointment and contempt. Finally, it takes up residence in a hovel near an apparently peaceable family. It watches and learns from this family. It greatly admires what it sees and hopes to visit them someday. It invests all its energy in this prospect—rehearsing, polishing its manners. The time arrives for its greeting, however, and the family brutally turns it away. Like a flash of dynamite, the monster's last vestige of faith in humanity is dashed. Its final plea for dignity is crushed. The agony of total rejection, the creature apprises us, gives "place to a hellish rage" (p. 126).

Rarely have such sentiments been portrayed more vividly, more disarmingly. Every fiber of the creature's existence—an existence formally designed to promote the social good—now tends toward mayhem. Every one of its already wondrous capacities—speed, strength, agility, endurance—magnify now as they totally disavow constraint. We are introduced, in these scenes, to the most tumultuous regions of our psyches. Nothing can surpass the unbridled fury of this creature, nothing!—which is precisely why it has awed us for so many generations. What we can also see here is that the most *pronounced* excesses (e.g., rage, frenzy) arise not from fulfillment and bliss but from trauma and desperation (see Schneider 1990). Walton's enthusiasm and Frankenstein's zeal, for example, are "child's-play" compared with the cataclysmic ardor of the unconsoled creature. To be sure, this ardor is unproductive, for it is too explosive to be harnessed. But it is an instructive glimpse into who and what we can become and how much more there is to discover about ourselves.

The subtitle of *Frankenstein,* "The Modern Prometheus," becomes clearer now as we ponder the above themes. How far can a human being go in acquiring god-like powers? What is the price of creative zeal, disillusionment? What kind of a God permits such extremities?

Frankenstein is a tale of hyperexpansion. It is a discourse on the gradual embracing of chaos and proceeds at several levels. The first level is that of curiosity, exploration, and experimentation; this is the level at which Walton and Frankenstein *begin* their projects. The second level is that of ambition and creation; this is the level at which the two protagonists *realize* their dreams. Both of these levels are associated with a sense of acceptance, a sense that their actions are socially or cosmically *justified*. Walton, for example, finds his justification in the earth sciences, Frankenstein, in the biological sciences and in the distinct sense (hope?) that divinity is "on his side." In time, however, it becomes clear that, at least in Frankenstein's case, he is "in over his head." He fails to anticipate an entire chain of eventualities—his (and the world's) inability to tolerate the creature's hideousness; the creature's indignation over this intolerance; the creature's capacity for vengeance; his own fruitless pursuit of the creature. Step by step, Frankenstein's world unravels. Step by step he is drawn (and projects himself) into circumstances beyond his control. This failure, on the part of Frankenstein, to anticipate the implications of his actions is the novel's third level of expansion (or more properly, hyperexpansion, because it is dysfunctional). Hyperexpansion reaches its zenith, finally, in what is implied about the *ultimate* creator, the one which tacitly assents to Frankenstein's calamity. "Yea, He is more terrible and frightful than the devil," Luther (quoted in Otto 1958, p. 99) aptly observes,

> For He dealeth with us and bringeth us to ruin with power, smiteth and hammereth us and payeth no heed to us . . . In His majesty He is a consuming fire. . . . For therefrom can no man refrain: if he thinketh on God aright, his heart in his body is struck with terror . . . Yea, as soon as he heareth God named, he is filled with trepidation and fear.

41

Smaller and Smaller (1956), M. C. Escher. © 1956 M. C. Escher/Cordon Art, Baarn, Holland.

Part III
Further Inquiries
into Wisdom-Horror

*They who dream by day are cognizant of
many things which escape those who
only dream by night. In their gray
visions they obtain glimpses of eternity,
and thrill, in awakening, to find that
they have been on the verge of the great
secret.*

—EDGAR ALLAN POE

We have now examined two archetypal excursions into
hyperconstrictive and hyperexpansive horror, *Dracula* and *Frankenstein* respectively. While these tales are by no means thematical-
ly exhaustive, they do represent seminal contributions to our
understanding of the human condition. Next, we will broaden
our inquiry by pursuing somewhat lesser esteemed, but nonethe-
less classic, counterparts to *Dracula* and *Frankenstein*. These have
been grouped according to their lineage: further studies in
hyperconstriction—*The Phantom of the Opera*, "The Fall of the
House of Usher," *The Invisible Man*, and *The Incredible Shrinking
Man*; further studies in hyperexpansion—*Dr. Jekyll and Mr. Hyde*,
The Birds, and *Forebidden Planet*; and inquiries into bipolar
(hyperconstrictive *and* hyperexpansive) horror—*Vertigo* and
Alien. I have chosen these stories, derived from both books and
films, on the basis of their popularity, general critical acclaim,
and my personal preference. Each, in its own way, adds to and
elaborates upon this book's central thesis, which here bears
repeating: (1) the basis for ecstasy and terror is constrictive/
expansive infinity (or the holy); (2) terror sets the upper limit on

ecstasy, and not vice versa; and (3) the *encounter* with this limit, rather than its denial or passive acceptance, promotes vitality and social sensitivity. Once again, I suggest that you read or view the works before considering my treatment of them. Let us continue, then, with the hyperconstrictive lineage of *Dracula*.

Further Studies in Hyperconstriction

*He meddled in things men should leave
alone.*

—FROM *THE INVISIBLE MAN*
(1933 FILM VERSION)

The Phantom of the Opera

Gaston Leroux's *Phantom of the Opera* (1911/1987) is a story about a disfigured, ghostly musician who terrorizes the late-nineteenth century Paris Opera House. The story opens with the dramatic and unexpected death of a stage-hand hanging in the Opera House rafters. Soon, we are introduced to the arresting diva Christine Dee, who appears to have been mysteriously tutored by the Phantom or, as she calls him, the "angel of music." The balance of the story revolves around Christine's curious romantic involvement with the Phantom (in part due to his unrelenting pursuit of her) and her growing love for the youthful Raoul. The story intensifies as the Phantom becomes violently jealous of Raoul and is implicated in more and more Opera House mischief. The book closes, finally, with the dramatic kidnapping of Christine (by the Phantom) during one of her performances. Infuriated and lovelorn, Raoul and a man known as "the Persian" (who has valuable knowledge about the Phantom) fight their way into the Phantom's labyrinthine hide-out under the Opera House and attempt to rescue the diva. They are unsuccessful, however, managing only to fall prey to his tormenting pranks, such as the bewildering "palace of mirrors." By showing the Phantom that he can be loved despite his revolting ugliness, however, Christine prompts him to "let go" of his captives and permit them to live out their respective destinies. The Phantom (who calls himself "Erik"), dies uneventfully in the Opera House underground.

Lon Chaney as the Phantom of the Opera. From *The Phantom of the Opera*, Universal, 1925. Copyright © by Universal City Studios, Inc. Courtesy of MCA Publishing Rights, a division of MCA Inc.

As can be seen, *The Phantom of the Opera* parallels the hyperconstrictive dreadfulness of *Dracula.* The Phantom, for example, is a devious, shadowy figure who preys upon the innocent and unwary; his environment is dark and concealed, far from the everyday world (he, too, sleeps in a coffin). He is cunning and relies heavily on surprise and subtle manipulation. Despite his perverseness, however, he is an object of much curiosity, and like Dracula, he is a complex figure who can surpass almost anyone within his realm of knowledge.

But there are important differences between the two antagonists as well. Dracula has significantly greater destructive power than the Phantom (recall the former's capacity to materialize at will and his lifetimes of development); the Phantom, by contrast, is only capable of relatively local trickery and relatively modest destructiveness. Second, *The Phantom of the Opera* adds to and elaborates upon several *Dracula* motifs; these include the psycho-physiological experiences of descent, entrapment, bewilderment, and deterioration. Let us explore each of these dimensions more closely.

The Experience of Descent in *Phantom*

The sensation of being lowered, of falling, of losing one's grip, of slipping into an abyss, are given fresh interpretations in *Phantom.* Repeatedly, we are entranced by references to "trap-doors," "black holes," "whirlpools," and "winding" staircases (pp. 89, 110, 121). The Phantom is a "trap-door lover," the Persian quips at one point (p. 185). Christine admonishes Raoul about venturing into the Phantom's domain: "Never should you go there! . . . everything that is underground belongs to him!" (p. 110). At another moment, she catches Raoul, afraid that he will "disappear down the black hole" of the Opera House's substructure (p. 110). Leroux, finally, speaks of "peering into the darkness and the silence" of the Phantom's lair and of its "enormous corridors" (pp. 198–99).

Beyond the obvious intrauterine symbolism here, the connotations are chilling. What might it be like, we wonder, to "peer into" a seemingly bottomless pit, "a spiral stair into the very heart of the earth" (p. 121)? What would it be like to *fall* into such an enclosure? How *far* might one fall? What might it be like at the very *depths* of the earth, the universe, or the subconscious mind? Are we not haunted by such concerns when we stand upon cliffs, mountains, or tall buildings? Are we not drawn to such abysses in times of loneliness and despair? Far from being reveries of infancy, these are fundamental questions about living.

The Experience of Entrapment in *Phantom*

There is a distinct sense of confinement throughout *Phantom*. No one is safe, no one can escape, so long as the Phantom is at large. "I am everywhere" he says (p. 208). His underground is tailor-made for victimization. How does it feel, for example, to be relentlessly overheard, watched, and preyed upon? What is it like to stumble blindly to one's death or to await imminent catastrophe? And if you are Christine, what is it like to feel "surrounded by darkness" and "imprisoned . . . for love" (pp. 120, 124)? Or, if you are the Persian, what is the experience of being "seized . . . by the neck" and dragged far into the depths of the underground lake (p. 203)? What can be said for the victims of the Phantom's "incredible skill in the art of strangulation" (p. 218)? We are bombarded by such queries.

In the closing scene, Raoul and the Persian amble through innumerable corridors, passageways, and canals. They are hemmed in by walls, tiny and awkward enclosures, heavy air. Leroux captures their predicament and the quintessence of feeling trapped: "The darkness was thick around them, the silence heavy and terrible" (p. 200).

The Experience of Bewilderment in *Phantom*

Some people say that the further one probes the world of subtlety and detail, the more it begins to look like the world of vastness and immensity. At the same time that our purview narrows and focuses, it may also begin to acquire maddening intricacies and perplexities. We may lose all orientation. Such is the fate of all those who enter the Phantom's universe, while they remain alive.

The Phantom, Leroux informs us, compensated for his ugliness by plunging into hidden and elusive realms, by becoming a "conjurer" (p. 212). While others devoted themselves to worldly pursuits, he made a career of trickery. So driven was he to become great, to *matter* in some way, regardless of how macabre, that he curtailed no impulse and maintained no sense of propriety in the service of those who would employ him. We have already spoken of his brilliant knowledge of trap-doors and surprise attacks, but we will now consider his gift for deceiving. Raoul observes Christine in her dressing room mirror at one moment, and poof!—she is gone the next. Christine is singing along stupendously, and boom!—the stage goes black; when the lights return, she is gone. But there is perhaps no greater trickery, no larger puzzlement, than that daunting little room known as the "palace of mirrors." As Raoul comes to find out and the Persian already knew, this room is the embodiment of fragmentation, of harrowing penetrations into indefiniteness and illusion. The Persian recollects:

> The room in which [Raoul] and I were imprisoned was a regular hexagon, lined entirely with mirrors. . . . A decorative object, such as a column . . . was placed in one of the corners and immediately produced a hall of a thousand columns; for thanks to the mirrors, the real room was multiplied by six hexagonal rooms, each of which, in its turn, was multiplied indefinitely. (p. 228)

"The walls of this strange room," the Persian elaborated, "gave [one] nothing to lay hold of, because, apart from the solid decorative object, they were simply furnished with mirrors . . ." (p. 229).

Rarely has the horrific been portrayed more grippingly, more palpably. We are thrust by this passage into the fractionated world of subtlety and minutiae. We have no moorings in this world, no means of orientation. All we can do is collapse.

The Experience of Deterioration in *Phantom*

The theme of deterioration is given vivid attention in *Phantom*. There are numerous passages which allude to death, decay, dankness, and decomposition. Primal overtones abound. The Phantom, for example, is a "pale" figure with two "holes" for eyes and virtually nothing for a nose (pp. 9, 101). His face is portrayed as a "death's head" (p. 114). He is described as bony, skeleton-like, and "thin" (p. 9). One sometimes has the feeling that he half exists or that he can fade into and out of existence.

His dwelling is the quintessence of decay. One can almost touch the cobwebs and the heavy, stale air. The stench from the underground lake is palpable, and rotting bodies (the Phantom's victims) line the corridors.

The Phantom's emotional life also reflects corruption. He is damaged, isolated. He strikes out at the world because inside he "weeps" (p. 124). His guilt is crushing. He "accuses himself," "curses himself," and "implores" Christine to forgive him (p. 124). He "crawls" and grovels at her feet (p. 124). The Persian intimates that, inside, the Phantom is a "child"—riddled with self-hate. This is why he "relinquished everything above the surface of the earth" (p. 261).

The tragic story of Erik (the Phantom of the Opera) adds to and elaborates upon the hyperconstrictive horrors set forth in *Dracula*. It is a story about descent, entrapment, bewilderment, and deterioration. Erik is our nightmarish depth, our menacing "shadow." He is a secret part of many of us, locked away, hidden from the light. The underworld that he inhabits is a place where we might feel putrid, imperceptible and ineffectual, but it can be a place to cultivate secrets, fantasies, and intricate creations. Indeed, with his "extraordinary gifts of dexterity and imagination," this is precisely what Erik nurtured (p. 261). He compensated for his "ugliness" by becoming a virtuoso musician, magician, and ventriloquist. He mastered the art of engineering and roamed and eventually learned to rule the underworld. But he employed his brilliance in the service of revenge, and this is what made him so dismaying. He was too far gone, too deeply wounded, too enmeshed in occult practices to turn his life around. At the end, mercifully, he achieved a grain of self-respect (due to Christine's generosity) and lifted himself (and others) part-way out of the festering wound of self-reproach. However, one can never forget his excesses, nor the flair with which he produced them.

"The Fall of the House of Usher"

Edgar Allan Poe's "The Fall of the House of Usher" (1839/ 1981) is marked by one overriding sentiment: claustrophobia.

Mark Damon as Philip Winthrop in *The House of Usher*, American International Pictures, 1960. Copyright © by Universal City Studios, Inc. Courtesy of MCA Publishing Rights, a division of MCA Inc.

Claustrophobia, in this case, is not merely a fear of being enclosed but of being "closed in upon," surrounded, engulfed. The tale proceeds thus:

A curious traveler—the narrator—is summoned to the house of his boyhood friend, Roderick Usher. The setting is "dull, dark and soundless," and the "clouds hung oppressively low" (p. 199). "I know not what it was," the narrator tells us, "but with the first glimpse of [Usher's house], a sense of insufferable gloom pervaded my spirit" (p. 199). He then greets us with a series of foreboding images: The place was "stern" and "desolate" (p. 199). The walls were "bleak", the windows "vacant" (p. 199). "There was an iciness," the narrator continues, "a sinking, . . . an unredeemed dreariness of thought which no goading of the imagination could torture into . . . the sublime" (p. 199). In addition to these "sorrowful impressions," the house was bordered by "a black and lurid tarn" (p. 199).

The narrator gazes at the scene with a "shudder" (p. 199). Despite its eeriness, however, there was something "thrilling" about it, something "beyond our depth" (p. 199).

Summoned to aid Usher, who besides his sister is the last surviving member of the family, the narrator enters the dwelling. The "vivid force of the sensations [which] had oppressed" him on the outside were no less salient now that he was indoors (p. 200). "There hung an . . . atmosphere which had no affinity with the air of heaven, but which had reeked up from the decayed trees, and the grey wall, and the silent tarn—a pestilent and mystic vapor, dull, sluggish, faintly discernable, and leaden hued" (p. 200). Apart from a strange "fissure" and a few "crumbling stones," the house itself appeared to be intact. And yet the narrator was struck by the "wild inconsistency" of it all (p. 201).

After making his way "through many dark and intricate passages," he finally greets his friend, Roderick Usher (p. 201). Although formerly Usher was habitually and excessively reserved, the narrator finds Usher "cordial" (p. 201). Still, the more he gazes upon Usher and his surroundings, the more he breathes "an atmosphere of sorrow. An air of stern, deep, and irredeemable gloom," he elaborates, "hung over and pervaded all" (p. 201).

Finding his companion "wan" and "cadaverous," the narrator enjoins him to divulge his burdens (p. 202). These burdens, we find, are numerous and intensify the pall that so heavily looms. Usher, we discover, suffers from a "morbid acuteness of the senses" (p. 203). He is horrified by all but the mellowest sounds, he is repulsed by myriad textures and odors, and he tolerates but the faintest luminosity. "I *must* perish in this deplorable folly," he declares (p. 202). "In this . . . pitiable condition" he goes on, "I feel that the period will sooner or later arrive when I must abandon life and reason together, in some struggle with the grim phantasm, FEAR" (pp. 202). Usher's sister, meanwhile, also grapples with this specter; she is "wasting away" and suffers from periodic bouts of catalepsy (or "waxy" paralysis).

This "unceasing radiation of gloom" is no less evident in Usher's picture gallery (p. 203). One painting reveals a "long rectangular vault or tunnel, with low walls, smooth, white, and without interruption or device" (p. 204). This "excavation lay at an exceeding depth below the surface of the earth," and "no outlet" or "light" is observable "in any portion of its vast extent" (p. 204).

The basis for the Usher tragedy, however, appears to be in the "grey stones of the home" (p. 206). There is something about their "arrangement," Usher observes, something about the "decay" and "fungi" which "overspread them" and about their "reduplication" in the tarn, that has exerted a "terrible influence" on his family for centuries (p. 206).

As to just what this "influence" constitutes, neither Usher nor Poe, for that matter, are entirely clear. The home and land are tainted in some way. There is a "sentience" or consciousness about them that ever tightens its grip (p. 206). Not only do the walls creak, but psychological and physical disorder abound. Usher plays his guitar, eats bland food, and lives within "narrow limits" to temporarily stave off this condition, but it rapidly returns to haunt him (p. 204). By degrees, the narrator too, feels it "creeping upon" him (p. 208).

Days pass and the tormenting miasma worsens. "Huge masses of agitated vapour . . . [hang] about and [enshroud] the mansion" (p. 209). Strange "grating sounds" are heard in the direction of the family crypt, where Madeline (Usher's sister) is freshly entombed (p. 210). This comingling of events so unnerves

Usher that he voices a startling revelation: *"We have put her living in the tomb"* (p. 211)! He "heard her first feeble movements in the . . . coffin . . . days ago," he laments, "yet [he] . . . *dared* not speak!" (p. 211). Remote sounds now turn piercing. Usher's eyes are "bent fixedly before him, and throughout his whole countenance there [reigns] a stone rigidity" (p. 211). Suddenly, Madeline appears. "Bloody and emaciated," she falls "heavily inward upon the person of her brother, and . . . [strikes] him to the floor a corpse" (p. 211).

The narrator hurriedly takes leave of the mansion and watches "the deep and dank tarn at [his] feet [close] sullenly and silently over the fragments of the HOUSE OF USHER" (p. 212).

The fears of being closed in upon, engulfed, and obliterated are the chief preoccupations in "Usher." From the outset, we are bombarded by claustrophobic imagery—clouds, darkness, oppression. The house is forbidding, its occupants are suspicious and reticent. We wend our way, both literally and figuratively, through many encircling passages, vaults, and "atmospheres." There is a distinct feeling of corruption about the house, that it is rotting from within and without. While aspects of this corruption are tangible—for example, the decaying trees, crumbling stones, and bizarre illnesses—other features are less palpable. Echoes of ancestral incest and madness abound. Gaseous vapors, and above all, the tarn, lap menacingly at the dwelling's perimeter. There is reproval in the air, a kind of willful cosmic payback. Taken together, these occurrences form a living miasma of corruption, slowly ensnarling and smothering those within its grasp.

Yet, as the narrator points out, there is also something "thrilling" about this miasma, at least initially. The earth and house associate with the magic, power, and primal energies that give rise to life.

In the end, "Usher" is more than a graphic tale about this or that disease or adversity but a commentary on all diseases, all adversities. It is a yarn about that vast, undecipherable mystery called Being and its all-enveloping power. We are thrown into it, dissolved by it.

"And the deep and dank tarn . . . close[s] sullenly and silently over the fragments of". . . *ourselves.*

The Invisible Man *(1933 film version)*

Invisibility is a very unsettling concept. Not only does it evoke the horrors of *self*-dissolution but of the dissolution of *things*—the unseen and undetectable. H. G. Wells's *Invisible Man* is a classic meditation on the latter.

The 1933 film version opens, appropriately enough, with miniscule but assaultive imagery—a turbulent snowstorm. A howling wind teases us with its malevolence. Soon, a strange man with dark glasses and a bandaged head makes his appearance. He trudges through the storm and comes upon a small English pub. The patrons there are aghast, having little capacity to assimilate the odd caller.

That caller, it turns out, is a brilliant, eccentric chemist named Dr. Griffin. He has arrived there to find a room and carry out a mysterious experiment. Although he is supplied with such a room, he is extremely curt to his hosts. He insists on absolute privacy and becomes increasingly belligerent towards them.

Meanwhile, Griffin's disappearance from his usual circle prompts his colleagues, Drs. Kemp and Cranley, to grow concerned. Kemp suggests that Griffin is a romantic and that he became a victim of his own irresponsible creations: Griffin "meddled in things men should leave alone," Kemp snaps. Cranley's daughter Flora, on the other hand, is sympathetic to Griffin and protests these accusations.

Griffin's clash with the innkeeper, meantime, reaches the "boiling point." Unable to maintain his solitude and thus complete the experiment that would render him visible, Griffin lunges at and violently repels the innkeeper. Soon afterward, an unassuming but determined police constable shows up at Griffin's door and attempts to subdue him. The scientist will not yield, however, and dramatically exposes his condition of invisibility. The constable reaches for him but to no avail; the invisible Griffin pounces on the officer and mercilessly throttles his neck.

Intriguing at first, Griffin's invisibility becomes increasingly diabolical. By degrees, the scientist grows intoxicated with his condition and the catastrophic consequences it has for humankind. "An invisible man can rule the world!" Griffin bellows. "Nobody will see him come. Nobody will see him go. He can hear *every* secret. He can rob and rape and kill!"

Claude Rains as the Invisible Man, with Gloria Stewart as Flora. From *The Invisible Man,* Universal, 1933. Copyright © by Universal City Studios, Inc. Courtesy of MCA Publishing Rights, a division of MCA Inc.

In time, Griffin is totally consumed by megalomania. He demands that Kemp assist him in making "the world grovel" at their feet. Kemp refuses, however, and enlists the aid of Cranley and Flora to discourage Griffin's plans. Flora visits Griffin but fails to move him. "I wanted to do something tremendous," Griffin explains to her, "to achieve what men of science have dreamt of since the world began. I was so pitifully poor," he goes on, "I had nothing to offer you, Flora. I was just a poor, struggling chemist." But "I shall offer my secret to the world," he cries with a vengeance, "with all its terrible power. . . . The nation that wins my secret can sweep the world with invisible armies!"

Soon after this diatribe, the police arrive, and Griffin knows that Kemp has betrayed him. "Believe me," he confronts Kemp, "as surely as the moon will set and the sun will rise, I shall kill you tomorrow night. I shall kill you even if you hide in the deepest cave of the earth."

Griffin again eludes the police and "roams the countryside at will." "The invisible man has been reported in a hundred different places," an exasperated officer laments. And sure enough, Griffin does kill Kemp at the appointed hour. He robs, assaults, and humiliates many more before his own appointment with fate. Late one evening, as snow falls and winds swirl, Griffin glides invisibly into a barn and falls asleep at the foot of a haystack. In the morning, a farmer overhears a rustling sound where Griffin lay. A large contingent of police are alerted, and they smoke Griffin out of the barn. Footprints begin to appear in the snow, and they shoot the desperate specter squarely in the lungs. Just before he dies, however, Griffin acknowledges his folly: "I failed," he whispers to Flora. "I meddled in things that man must leave alone."

The Invisible Man carries us one step further into hyperconstrictive dread. It is an excursion into microscopic terror, not unlike that which is implied by insects, disease, and various forms of pollution. Griffin is a violent, unpredictable force. You never know where he is lurking, what he is observing, or when he will strike. He's like a wild, sprawling virus.

The product of a brilliant scientific experiment, Griffin's invisibility is fascinating at first. How it could aid humanity! What it could reveal about the chemical and physical composition of matter! For this prospect to come to fruition, however, it would require every faculty that Griffin lacks: discipline, control, caution. Griffin, on the other hand, is intemperate, vengeful, and alarmingly maniacal.

To be sure, the drug that produces Griffin's invisibility has maddening effects, but his feelings of worthlessness emphatically reinforce this condition. He was a lowly chemist, he explains, but now he has unmatchable power. He was dismissable once, but now people will "grovel" at his feet. Like so many of the monsters we have described, Griffin's indignation takes us to the very edge of his condition, the very pinnacle of his specialness.

On the one hand, Griffin is hyperexpansive. His grandiosity and his pretensions to dominate are a direct result of his former perceptions of smallness. But unlike the developments in *Frankenstein,* this is *not* the horrific thrust of *Invisible Man;* the emphasis, by contrast, is on Griffin's *vehicle* for his reprisals— namely, the capability of invisible stealth, and the chilling, otherworldly associations that this transformation has to the microbial world. In addition to the occult forces we have already mentioned, these associations run to such more obscure fields as spirits, witchcraft, and sheer, formless space.

The Incredible Shrinking Man *(1957 film version)*

The dread of *becoming* infinitesimal (rather than dread of infinitesimal things per se) is the distinctive feature of Richard Matheson's *Incredible Shrinking Man* (1957).

What might it be like, the film inquires, if a human being faced irreversible diminishment? What would the person's experience be like? What mental and physical challenges would he or she face, and how would he or she cope with these challenges? Although marred by an upbeat, thoroughly incongruous ending, the film is a riveting study of the diminution of one's being.

Exposed to some strange form of radiation, an ordinary if slightly arrogant man, Robert Scott Carey, begins to shrink in size. He first notices the shrinkage in relation to his oversize trousers. Next, he observes that his shirt is too big. After several visits to a physician, his worst nightmare is confirmed: his shrinking is real and it is *unstoppable.*

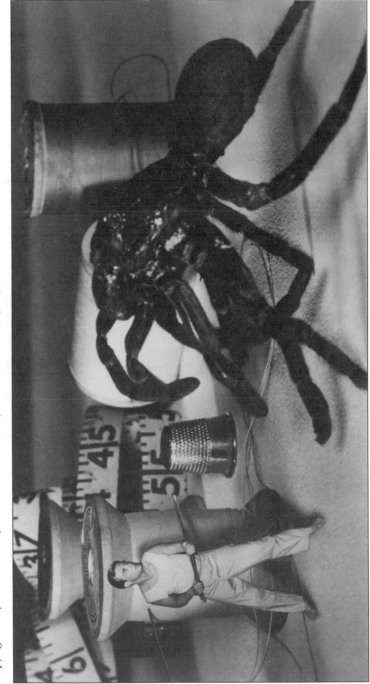

Grant Williams as the Incredible Shrinking Man. From *The Incredible Shrinking Man*, Universal-International, 1957. Copyright © by Universal City Studios, Inc. Courtesy of MCA Publishing Rights, a division of MCA Inc.

Gradually, but at a sustained pace, Carey's world narrows. He and his wife Louise have hope, but it is persistently dashed. "As long as you have this wedding ring on" Louise assures Carey, "you've got me." The next moment Carey's ring slips ominously from his finger. As his condition progresses, Carey plunges further and further into microcosmic despair. Old relationships to objects—doors, chairs, stairs, the family cat—become daunting and the objects themselves unwieldy or dangerous. Carey gradually feels less like a man and more as a toy in a universe of giants. It's "easy enough to talk about soul and spirit and essential worth," Carey observes, "but not when you're three feet tall."

For all its horrific debasement, there is something captivating about Carey's condition. He is a "curiosity." The news media clamor for stories about him. A voyeuristic crowd gathers outside his home. A circus offers him employment. What entrances people so? Something about the relativity of perspective plays a role here. What is it like, we wonder, to see the world in greatly enhanced detail? How does it feel to be so remote and so estranged from the world in its familiar perspective? Do such little creatures, relatively insignificant, have hidden powers and influences? They must have, we surmise, because they are privy to incalcuable living and inanimate subtleties, hidden strengths and vulnerabilities (the film *Freaks* is also relevant in this context).

Unable to halt his diminution, Carey narrowly escapes the claws of his now-lethal cat. He then stumbles into an ordinary packing box in his basement. "Its walls," he reports, "enclosed me like some gigantic pit." He then pokes his head out and gazes up at the basement steps, which "rise above [him] cliff by cliff."

After climbing out of the packing box, Carey surveys his "basement universe:" "The cellar floor stretched before me like some vast, primeval plane, empty of life, littered with the relics of a vanished race." This "bleak" chasm is so foreign to Carey, so radically "other" to his former life, that he must now renounce that life altogether.

Formerly commonplace objects—a matchbox, a sewing needle, a bit of food—presently become formidable resources, tools in the unremitting battle for survival. Once-minor annoyances —a mouse-trap, a dollop of paint, a spider—now acquire threatening proportions.

The terrifying extremity of Carey's world is highlighted by a sudden leak in the basement boiler. Awash in a sea of turbulent water, Carey frantically battles for his life; in stark contrast, Carey's brother Charlie (who presumes Carey died hours earlier) calmly walks over to the leaking boiler and shuts it off. At the heel of Charlie's colossal shoe, Carey shouts in vain for assistance.

As time passes, however, Carey's perspective begins to shift yet again, and this is where the story, in my opinion, veers meekly away from its trajectory (see also Clarens, 1968). "A strange calm possessed me," Carey informs us. "[I felt] as if my mind were bathed in a brilliant light."

After Carey subdues "every fear fused into one hideous, night-black horror" (the spider), he begins to turn mystical. He reports that he no longer feels "hunger" or drive or the "terrible fear of shrinking." He continues to dissolve into the infinitesimal, but he has a "profound" realization: It's *okay*. The infinitely small and the infinitely large, he reports, are really just "two ends of the same concept . . . [that] eventually meet, like the closing of a gigantic circle."

Hence, what had formerly "stretched endlessly before" him, what had been "deep, dark, mysterious, and dangerous," was now "closed," illuminated, and secure; what was formerly night-black horror is now simply an alteration of perspective, one aspect of a grand, consoling unity; what had once felt "absurd," now brims with clarity and meaning. In one majestic moment, Carey totally surrenders to the powers that be and accepts his fate. He even accepts the prospect of obliteration, because "to God," Carey waxes rhapsodically, "there is no zero."

Shrinking Man is a spellbinding journey into the microcosm. Not only is it an incredibly life-like adventure; it is an evocative one as well. What challenges does Carey's world hold, the film inquires, and how might he (or we) cope with them?

Although wondrous at first, Carey's predicament rapidly turns macabre. His diminishment acquires *alarming* proportions. He faces *unstoppable* alterations of experience. That these extremities dismay, however, is significantly lost with the film's ending, which is a letdown; the ending showers us with metaphysical hope but on what basis? Carey's problem is bottomless, indefinite; the film's ending, however, is unifying, secure. Carey's condition is not just a link in a prescribed chain of being; it is a link without anchor, an *endless,* unconsoling spiral.

By conceiving of his condition as a part of some larger, supportive whole (God), Carey does not so much accept as *give up* on his bewildering plight. In the place of *tremendum* he now observes *placidity;* in the place of *mystery* he now experiences *faith.*

But faith and placidity in this case are constrictive. They imply prematurely that what we see at the end of the film—sunshine, friendly creatures, vegetation—is representative of Carey's present and future possibilities. By contrast, everything poignant about Carey's journey (until the ending) resists such a characterization. A more consistent portrayal would suggest that not only light but also darkness will saturate Carey's universe—it will be a world of bizarre and exotic organisms, whizzing microscopic forms, and *countless* fragmentations beyond.

The film's finale, however, in its own right, *is* poignant. It betrays the degree to which we demand reassurance in this world and the baselessness against which that demand is forged.

We have now considered five explorations of the infinitesimal: *Dracula, Phantom of the Opera,* "The Fall of the House of Usher," *The Invisible Man,* and *The Incredible Shrinking Man.* Each highlights a significant facet of hyperconstriction. *Dracula* emphasizes concealment and surrender; *Phantom* dwells on descent, entrapment, bewilderment, and deterioration; *House of Usher* accents encirclement; *Invisible Man* focuses on the dissolution of things; and *Shrinking Man* stresses dissolution of the self.

Each of these facets dovetails with our thesis. Specifically, they each evoke a simultaneous sense of the marvelous and the terrible. They imply that *infinity* (or in this case, the *infinitesimal*) is the basis for these marvels and terrors. Except for *Shrinking Man,* they suggest that the marvelous is circumscribed, the terrible unbound; and they imply that the encounter with this microcosmic context, rather than denial or passive acceptance of this context, promotes well-being.

Let us now return to and explore the hyperexpansive lineage of *Frankenstein.*

The First
Probe (1979),
Robert W.
Vanderhorst.

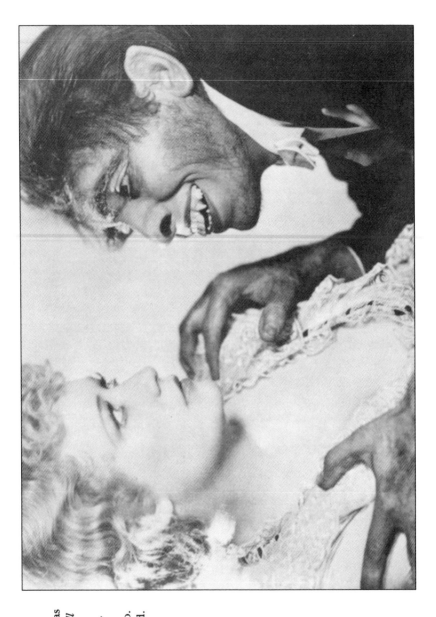

Fredric March as
Mr. Hyde, with
Miriam Hopkins as
Ivy. From *Dr. Jekyll
and Mr. Hyde*,
Paramount, 1932.
© 1932 Turner
Entertainment Co.
All rights reserved.

Further Studies in Hyperexpansion

Oh God, . . . I have trespassed on your
domain. Forgive me, help me.

—FROM *DR. JEKYLL AND MR. HYDE*
   (1932 FILM VERSION)

Dr. Jekyll and Mr. Hyde *(1932 film version)*

Ever since *Frankenstein,* numerous yarns have been spun about
the perils of human presumption, in which the themes of desire,
greed, lust, and ambition have acquired alarming dimensions.
Standing singularly proud among the exemplars which boast
these phenomena is Robert Louis Stevenson's *Dr. Jekyll and Mr.
Hyde.*

The 1932 film version of *Jekyll and Hyde* is particularly
noteworthy. Focusing, as it does, on the sexual and aggressive
components of the Frankenstein legacy, the film is a supreme
indictment of both conventional and libertine innocence.

Enter Dr. Henry Jekyll, stolid, well-bred, and reputable . . .
but these are merely his surface traits. At another level, Jekyll is
impassioned, sensual, and fiery. He is a dutiful professor yet one
who pronounces extravagant theoretical positions. He is a
gentlemanly companion to his beloved Muriel, yet he openly
acknowledges his lustiness. A man of contradictions, Jekyll is rife
with tension. "The soul of man is not truly one but truly two," he
shares with his students one day—the "good" or noble and the
"bad" or animalistic. Because these disharmonies are so painful,
Jekyll anticipates a time when "the two selves could be separated
from one another." "How much freer the good in us would be,"
he goes on. "What heights it might scale. And the so-called evil
would fulfill itself and trouble us no more."

Indeed, Jekyll has been experimenting with this theory for

some time, we learn. The more he *expresses* his two sides, he seems to find, the freer each is to go its own way: his noble nature is less distracted by instinctual urges and his animalistic side is freer of guilt. But Jekyll has not even come close to completing his study; he must considerably widen its scope—especially in investigating his "wilder" nature. He turns to Muriel, for example, and says: "Before, I was drawn to the mysteries of science, the unknown. But now the unknown wears *your* face." After being taken to task by Muriel's father for pressing for an "early" wedding date, Jekyll defiantly rebukes him. Dr. Lanyon, Jekyll's colleague, then admonishes Jekyll for his intemprance, his lack of "sobriety."

But "I'm not marrying to be sober," Jekyll protests, "I'm marrying to be drunk, drunk with love and life and experiments!"

"There are bounds beyond which one should not go," warns Lanyon.

Jekyll snaps back: "I tell you, there are no bounds, Lanyon!"

"You ought to control [your] instincts," Lanyon reiterates.

"We may control our actions but not our impulses," Jekyll rebutts.

What we see here, then, is that, despite Lanyon's objections and the objections of Victorian culture, Jekyll is increasingly direct. The more he can "fulfill" (and hence, "siphon off") his animal nature, the less remorseful and desperate he becomes and the more he becomes a pure and liberated being.—At least this is what Jekyll perceives *thus far*. But Lanyon's warnings may yet have merit: there may, indeed, be uncrossable "bounds."

Jekyll faces the first major test of his theory unexpectedly. On a dark, forbidding street-corner, he observes a man molesting a woman. The virtuous physician rushes up to the perpetrator and pushes him aside. He then follows the victim to her apartment and attempts to comfort her. Although the woman, a local barmaid named Ivy, is grateful for his help, she also quickly becomes infatuated with him. She shows him a bruise on her thigh. She undresses on the pretext of allowing him a better view of her "injuries." Finally, in an all-out attempt to entice him, she throws her garter belt at him. Jekyll is tittilated but steadfastly professional. The pivotal moment occurs, however, as Jekyll exits. Teasingly swinging her legs, Ivy's image is softly superimposed on the screen. Her voluptuous, inviting body *lingers* in his thoughts.

We are now thrust into Jekyll's lab. Chemicals and test tubes abound. A water-filled cauldron begins to simmer. In a fit of passion, Jekyll prepares a formula and guzzles it down. A dream-like swoon overtakes him. Images crowd his mind. He sees his girlfriend Muriel insisting that he "wait" for her father to set their wedding date. He abruptly switches to Ivy and sees her sensual, swinging legs. He begins grunting and growling, becoming the pure beast he so longs to fulfill. Finally, he is transformed! Stretching as if to touch the sky, he cries, *"Free!* Free at last!" "You hypocrites," he goes on, "you deniers of life. If you could see me now!" And the cauldron above his fireplace boils over.

Jekyll now meets his supreme test, the culmination of his work—a separated, pure animalism, the total unshackling of desire. But will it truly liberate him? And will it assuage remorse?

Darting about at a frightening pace, the being whom we now call "Hyde" sets out in search of Ivy. Spotting her at a local beer hall, Hyde is unabashed: "I want you," he declares, and "what I want I get." Although intrigued at first, Ivy soon becomes concerned. A customarily tough, aggressive "broad," Ivy abruptly turns genteel. Whereas Jekyll had once been the polite, reluctant one, Ivy now acquires these characteristics. Hyde is beyond Ivy's bounds, in other words, beyond even the harsh, working-class grit of the beer-hall. "You *belong* to me," Hyde declares to Ivy.

The next day, Hyde transforms (with a chemical antidote) back to Jekyll. Life proceeds as usual except for one disturbing fact: Jekyll is preoccupied by Hyde. Indeed, he is obsessed with him, and he is increasingly fixated on Ivy as well. At the same time, he becomes perturbed. "I've played with dangerous knowledge," he reports to Muriel. "I've walked a strange and terrible road."

Jekyll's road becomes increasingly dangerous. Muriel and her father go on holiday, and Jekyll indulges nightly in "Hyde." Hyde, meanwhile, arranges for Ivy to live in an attractive London flat. She becomes his "kept woman" and plunges further into victimization. Hyde is indomitable. There is no in-between for him; he is maximally direct. If someone stands in his way, he blasts them aside; if he becomes jealous, he maims or even kills the rival; if he is lustful, he rapes.

For Jekyll, however, these eruptions begin to take their toll. In his "restored" hours, he becomes tortured by recollections of Hyde's mayhem. Upon Muriel's return, Jekyll vows to terminate Hyde, and hence, his experiment.

It is a clear, resplendent day. Weeks have passed since Jekyll's horrifying ordeals, and Muriel has convinced her father to set an early wedding date. Filled with buoyant thoughts, and with only traces of the torments of his former inquiries, Jekyll approaches a park bench. Joyously, he sets himself down and observes a bird chirping in a tree. "Thou wast not born for death, immortal bird," Jekyll shouts. "No hungry generations tread thee down." Suddenly, one of the most revelatory scenes in the film, indeed, in the entire horror genealogy, unfolds. A black cat darts across the tree limb and kills the bird. The mood and the tone of the picture abruptly darken. Jekyll's face turns dour. "Thou wast not born for death!" he sinisterly repeats. "But it *is* death!" he exclaims. "Death!" And Hyde leaps maniacally out from the bench.

The morbid and the chaotic cannot be transcended after all, Jekyll discovers. Invariably it looms, piercing into the unstained veneer. If he was skeptical about the efficacy of his theory before this incident, he was now totally disbelieving: Hyde was not only a regrettable memory but a condition—the reality of things. Once transgressed, the Hyde boundary, the boundary of unbridled will, could not be retreated from, nor could it be satisfactorily fulfilled; the unbridled will simply *consumes* and relentlessly vies for more.

Mercilessly, Hyde bursts into his unsuspecting mistress's chambers. "I'll give you a lover now," he bellows. "His name is *death!*" Shocked and disarmed, Ivy is as estranged from Hyde as Muriel is distant from Ivy and her rabble-rousing mob. Ivy had been sure that he had ceased; she had been sure that good and decent people had triumphed over him, had stemmed his tyranny; but she (like so many of us who over-idealize) was deluded.

"I'm going to let you into a secret," Hyde scintillates, "a secret so great that those who share it with me cannot live. *I* am the angel whom you wanted to slave for in love!" 'I am Dr. Jekyll' he intimates, and he proceeds to strangle her.

Hyde's anarchy then spreads hastily to his colleague Lanyon. Upon showing him the secret that "would stagger the devil himself," Hyde (who has now reverted to Jekyll) pleads for "help." "There is no help for you," Lanyon snaps. "You've committed the supreme blasphemy. . . . I told you that no man could violate the traditions of his kind and not be damned!" It's "too late," Lanyon goes on. "You cannot conquer it. It has conquered you."

Just before he is rounded up and destroyed by the police, Jekyll makes his final plea: "Oh God, I have trespassed on your domain. I have gone further than man should go. Forgive me, help me."

As with *Frankenstein, Jekyll* indicts both our propriety and expansive reaching out. Dr. Jekyll's quest for authenticity is justified. His culture is wound tight with rules, with feeble and arbitrary regulations. He is suppressed, oppressed, and choked off. He longs to be free, not only in spirit but also in body—especially body.

Although Muriel is the spark for his self-crusade, Ivy is the flame. She is the catalyst for his plunge into the orgiastic. At last, he proclaims, he will be "free!" At last, he can taste—without distraction or remorse—*both* his spiritual and sensual sides.

But the experiment misfires, of course. He neither separates nor purifies his dual natures. He becomes a mockery of liberation and finds his hyperexpansion as debilitating as his hyperconstriction. He can neither deliberate upon nor control his impulses; he can neither channel his energies nor be discrete. He becomes a driven, desiring machine.

But Hyde is no mere *Freudian* desiring machine. Beyond sexual craving, he symbolizes a far more daunting phenomenon —that of caprice, recklessness, and, ultimately, chaos. Like the cat who brutalizes the bird, Hyde brutalizes human civility.

Again we arrive at the "breaking point" of human striving. Whereas Frankenstein breached the limits of technical knowledge, Jekyll oversteps the horizons of sensual knowledge. That we need both these modes of human expression, there is little debate. But this is the key point: Frankenstein and Jekyll are uncompromising about their projects. They are unwilling to settle at certain points and give in to the powers that be. They are resistant, finally, to that crazy, quirky, human position—that of grasping for stars but of simultaneously groveling on earth.

The Birds *(1963 film version)*

For life is at the start a chaos in which one is lost. The individual suspects this, but he is frightened at finding himself face to face with this terrible reality, and tries to cover it over with a curtain of fantasy, where everything is clear. It does not worry him that his "ideas" are not true, he uses them as trenches for the defense of his existence, as scarecrows to frighten away reality.

—JOSE ORTEGA Y GASSET

"Frenzy" is defined by *Webster's New Collegiate Dictionary* (1988) as a "temporary madness, a violent mental or emotional agitation" (p. 492). For Alfred Hitchcock, who devoted his career to investigating the phenomenon, it is at the very core of the human problem. Not merely a master of suspense, Hitchcock is an artist of disruption, of the unleashing of chaos. In *Psycho,* this mentality found its expression through psychotic violence; in *Marnie,* through kleptomania; in *Rear Window,* through mutilation; and in *Vertigo,* through dizzying desire. Although *The Birds* contains elements of all four portrayals, it is a more general exercise in disorienting terror.

From the opening screen credits, foreshadowing in *The Birds* is superb: fragmented, disarrayed letters come together to form the names of the participants, and sinister bird silhouettes flitter about the screen. As the story unfolds, the camera pans to a cheerful, ordinary bird shop in downtown San Francisco. Melanie Daniels, an attractive—albeit unsettling—young woman, contemplates a purchase. There is something artificial about her. Her movements are tense and restricted. Passersby whistle at her, but she hardly blinks. The camera shifts to the outdoors

Tippi Hedren as
Melanie Daniels.
From *The Birds*,
Universal, 1963.
Copyright © by
Universal City
Studios, Inc.
Courtesy of MCA
Publishing Rights,
a division of MCA
Inc.

where an ominous flock of pigeons gather. Melanie is attracted to and meets a new customer in the shop, Mitch Brenner. He is a staid, somewhat aloof attorney, who seems both repelled and intrigued by her. Mitch is interested in purchasing "love-birds," and he half-believes Melanie's flirtatious play-acting as the store clerk. In typical Hitchcock fashion, their conversation is mocking, deceptive, and disquieting; each character reveals only so much and distorts or dodges significant information.

"Doesn't this make you feel awful," Mitch teases Melanie, "having all these poor, little, innocent creatures caged up like this?" "Well," Melanie sardonically replies, "we can't just let them fly around the shop, you know."

To this point, a gnawing suppression dominates the film. For all their playful banter, Melanie and Mitch are the quintessential modern couple—calculating, distant, restrained. A filmy veneer overlays their lives and is waiting to be dissolved or torn away.

Soon, we find Melanie purchasing love-birds (which Mitch was not able to acquire) to give to Cathy, Mitch's younger sister. Although Melanie does not know specifically where Mitch lives, she knows enough to track him down. She finds her way to Bodega Bay, a resort town about a hundred miles from San Francisco. Through a series of encounters, Melanie meets Cathy's teacher, Annie (who is also Mitch's ex-lover), and learns where Cathy and Mitch live.

Melanie proceeds to deliver her present to Cathy, and Mitch, who happens to be home, asks her to stay for the weekend. She agrees and soon accompanies Mitch on a boat ride across the Bay. They quietly glide along, when all of a sudden a gull swoops down and (almost "deliberately") pierces Melanie in the forehead. As the camera shot makes clear, the seal of smugness, of containment and suppression, is for the first time ruptured. The camera pans to Melanie's hand as she wipes away the blood; the stain glistens brightly on her pristine white glove.

Claiming falsely to Mitch that Annie is an old friend with whom she will stay the night, Melanie heads for her residence. When she arrives, however, Melanie is startled by Annie's intuition about her and Mitch. "Did something unexpected come up?" Annie asks, not without irony.

The next day, fresh cracks in the veneer of stability become apparent. The protagonists are positioned comfortably in

Mitch's home, but even among each other there is an underlying tension. Lydia, Mitch's mother, remarks that the chickens all over town do not seem to want to eat anything. Cathy, who is standing by Melanie as she plays the piano, discloses that Mitch's legal clients are very troublesome. "He has a client," she groans, "who shot his wife in the head six times, *can you imagine, six times!*"

We cut to Lydia, who is tersely critical of Mitch's choice of women. She corners Mitch and challenges him about a rumor she heard: Melanie "is the one who jumped into the fountain [naked] in Rome, isn't she?" "I think I can *handle* her," Mitch replies.

Gradually then, ingeniously, we are led into the vortex of disruption, of crimes and misdemeanors, of puzzling and unmanageable behavior. In time, we become increasingly perturbed. A dead bird drops inexplicably in front of Annie's doorstep. During a conversation with Mitch, Melanie explains how anguished she felt when she was "ditched" by her mother as a child. Cathy and her friends have a birthday party, and several birds attack them; balloons pop and glasses break in the tumult. Birds burst through Mitch's fireplace, break china, and dislodge a portrait of Lydia's late husband.

The police are alerted, but because they cannot find a "reason" for the occurrences they dismiss them. They are too strictly rational, Hitchcock implies, and clumsily overlook life's broader dimensions. The church, too, is a target of the indiscriminate birds and, by implication, Hitchcock's disdain: its windows have been smashed, its leaders are nowhere to be found.

In the next scene, Lydia drives over to a local farmer's home to purchase some chickens. When he fails to answer his door, she lets herself in—warily. Instantly, we face the symptoms of destabilization—broken china, shattered glass, toys strewn about the floor. As she (and we) proceed down a corridor, a palpable gloom fills the air. Suddenly, in five or six jolting sequences, the tragedy is unveiled. Lydia sees the farmer's battered body stretched across the floor of an adjacent room, his eyesockets streaming blood.

If the veil of containment has until this point only been frayed, it is now shredded. Lydia races home and begins "breaking down." Melanie tries to comfort her, but it is clear that little can help. "I don't think I can bear to be left alone," she whimpers. "I wish I was *stronger.*" Lydia's late husband Frank gave her strength, she intimates, he was always able to handle things; but he's gone, Lydia acknowledges, and beneath her smooth exterior (just as in Melanie's case), she feels adrift, lost at sea.

This scene is pivotal, for it clarifies Lydia's conflict with Melanie, and indeed, the conflict involving all those who compete for Mitch's attention. Lydia is dependent on Mitch, not for sexual or Oedipal reasons but for support, for a secure hold on her tenuous, broken existence.

In the next scene birds gather slowly in front of the nearby schoolhouse. Melanie approaches to warn the children and Annie (their teacher) of the impending danger. In typical Hitchcock fashion, however, Melanie is stymied in her efforts. Annie is leading the class in a sing-along and prompts Melanie to refrain, momentarily, from communicating. Without protest, Melanie removes to a bench on the nearby playground. One of the most deft touches in the history of cinema is now about to be displayed. As Melanie awaits the conclusion of the children's song, birds begin to collect on the "monkey gym" behind her. Simultaneously, the children can be heard singing a "round"—a song that is repeated and expanded indefinitely. The birds thus multiply and the song keeps extending, leaving one with the distinct sense that *everything*—not merely the airy habitations of the bird kingdom—is beginning to unravel. The birds, moreover, have now become symbolic. They illustrate the ever-widening potential for cataclysm that attends a commensurately widening human awareness.

Next, we shift to the town pub where Hitchcock antagonizes another "sacred cow"—science. The crowd at the pub is anxious and abuzz with news of the attacks. A prim elderly woman speaks to a few gossipers. "My avocation is ornithology," she declares, and the prospect of organized bird-attacks is "impossible." "Really," she demands, "let's be logical about this."

Moments later, a man is spotted at a gas station on the street below. He pauses, lights a cigarette, and unwittingly tosses the lit match into a pool of gasoline. This ignites an enormous fireball which threatens not only the gas station but several city blocks. The aged ornithologist observes helplessly as the conflagration spreads. Crowds pour onto the street, hysteria breaks forth. As though the flames were not enough, however, hordes of birds arrive, piercing and gouging their way through the crowd. Neither the innocent nor wary, witless nor wise are exempt from their fury.

Having escaped relatively intact thus far, Mitch and Melanie come upon another ghastly visage—that of Annie, hideously sprawled out on her front steps. Her body's position is conspicuously akin to that of a rape victim, except the violation in this case was not sexual, not animalistic per se, but otherworldly.

Upon their arrival back home, Mitch and Melanie find Cathy and Lydia "sick" with apprehension. The birds begin massing again, and Hitchcock's camera starts to tilt in kind. The complete derangement is under way.

Mitch musters every ounce of his remaining energy to prepare for the next attack. He boards up windows, reinforces furnishings, and barricades doorways. The house becomes a bulwark against calamity, which presses relentlessly from without. A sense of doom encircles the group, and in the flash of an instant, sharp pecking sounds hammer the walls. The pecking soon turns to a huge roar and the battering begins in earnest. Like a barrage of darts, birdbeaks split and poke their way through. Mitch works furiously to repair a shattered window and gravely slashes his arm. Stray birds careen aimlessly about, piercing and gouging at will. Everything is destabilizing—crashing, accelerating, breaking apart; everyone is running, dodging, emotionally unhinging.

Just as quickly, the barrage dissipates. While the others regroup and try to catch their breath, Melanie suddenly stirs to action. Mysteriously, she picks up a flashlight, ascends to the attic, and forces open the door, revealing their vulnerability to yet another barbarous attack. Melanie herself is now the subject of a vicious attack. It is of note here how relentless Hitchcock is, how inexhaustible his penchant for the deranged.

Although Mitch and his family are able to salvage her physically, Melanie is mentally asunder. The last scene parallels Melanie's state. Mitch opens the door of his house and unveils a decimated world. Swarms of gulls line the yard, driveway, and road. Miles of squawking crows clutch the telephone pole wires. The entire sky is pocked by anxious, fluttering wings. Mitch helps Melanie to her feet, and the four of them amble slowly, deliberately, carefully to his car. Just before they depart, Cathy's love-birds are conspicuously placed on the back seat. Amid the squeals of birds, confusion, and terror, the group rides off.

The Birds expands and extends the tumult dramatized by Hyde. Whereas Hyde (and Frankenstein's creation) are identifiable monstrosities, the birds suggests a cosmological motif—the natural catastrophes of living.

By basing the horror on the innocent and the ordinary, Hitchcock is able to highlight all that lies beyond these purviews, all that we resist. The harmless little love-birds, for example, are contrasted with the vulture-like gulls. Soaring crows are portrayed (as the film develops) as conniving predators. Graceful flutters turn into maniacal flapping. Small gatherings become great massings. Chirping noises turn into thunderous roars. Isolated pecks magnify into orgies of gouging. These are the rumblings, the crescendos of panic that course through Hitchcock's stuffy, contrived world.

Whereas *Hyde* counteracted the oppressiveness of the old order, *The Birds* counteracts the smugness of the new. Consider, for example, the "complacency"—the very word Hitchcock used to describe the film's thesis—of the opening scene (see Wood 1969, p. 137): the birdstore is flawlessly arranged and organized; each bird is placed safely in a cage; the clerk is poised and mannerly; Melanie is well-coiffed and neatly dressed; Mitch is fastidiously put together, polite, and diplomatic; dialogues among the participants are stilted; everyone plays a role and is interested in *convenience*—directness is shunned.

As disaster begins to intrude, no one is equipped to handle it. Even the authorities—*especially the authorities*—are unprepared. The police are too reasonable and the ornithologist is too dogmatic. There is little experimentalism in the town, little spontaneity.

The human characters in *The Birds,* then—like many of us—are complacent. They forget life's unruliness. They forget (or are afraid to acknowledge) that it is this very unmanageability that can enrich as well as petrify. It is this very disruptiveness that can spark vital relationships and bold reforms. (Consider, for example, the revolutionary epochs in art, science, politics, and indeed, in ordinary human relationships.) Acknowledgement of unruliness can also fortify us against hopeless despair. If we take it on faith, for example, that the world is a disorderly place, we are in a stronger position to account for and adapt to impending crises. Recall how Lydia, who took great pains to *deny* the tragic in her life, so readily collapsed in its midst.

The Birds, finally, is a film about chaos—the chaos within and without and the ability to encounter it, salvage what one can from it, and go on living in spite of it. The film's final stirring message is embodied by the love-birds. They are its symbols of hope. They represent that fragile middle ground, somewhere *between* the frantic and complacent.

Forbidden Planet *(1956 film version)*

Stories about outer space vivify the concept of boundlessness. They magnify earthly concerns and plunge us directly into what we both savor and dread. Space is the spectacular sea upon which all our lives depend. Within its fathomless chambers, we lead miniscule existences, with miniature and abbreviated glimpses of what it is that we are a part of. We aspire, we love, we fight, we fear; we think we are important; but all the while we are awash, suspended in a mystery.

Space is the culmination of everything that we are. The greater that we aspire, love, fight, fear—the *larger* our lives, the more intimate we become with the universe; this is because being human means being in relationship, and being in extended relationships means flirting with all that supports and surrounds us.

Forbidden Planet surveys these colossal themes. It examines humanity's widening mental and physical grasp and the consequences of both discovery and ambition.

Beyond the year A. D. 2200, the film informs us, humanity has pioneered far into the cosmos. Vehicles now exceeding the speed of light carry people to distant galaxies and remote forms of life. Presently, we pan to such a vehicle and its crew, whirring speedily through the galaxy. They are en route to planet Altair-4 to investigate the puzzling disappearence of a team of scientists.

Walter Pidgeon as Dr. Morbius, Leslie Nielsen as Captain Adams, and Ann Francis as Altaira. From *Forbidden Planet*, M-G-M, 1956. © 1956 Turner Entertainment Co. All rights reserved.

When the crew arrives on the planet, they are intrigued. Their surroundings are partly desert-like and partly lush. A green sky looms mysteriously overhead. Soon they meet Dr. Morbius, an inspiring professor of languages, who is also a brilliant inventor. Except for him and his daughter, Morbius conveys, the planet is uninhabited. The team of scientists he came with have all been annihilated, he continues, the result of some horrible, unknown force. These researchers were "torn limb from limb," he exclaims. Their ship was "vaporized." And yet Morbius and his daughter remained untouched. With these words, Morbius strongly advises the crew to leave the environs. But Captain John J. Adams, the leader of the crew, refuses, insisting that they must make a full inquiry.

The remarkable world of Altair-4 increasingly enchants the newly arrived crew. Romance (between Adams and Morbius' daughter, Altaira), technological wizardry, and a hospitable terrain brighten their days. In time, fresh excitements accrue. Adams and his first officer discover that Morbius has learned the secrets of an ancient, extinct civilization—the Krell—who once inhabited the planet. The Krell became so mentally and physically developed that they began to dispense with the material world. Their chief aim, so far as we can gather, was to free the mind from the body, from "instrumentation." They created machines that could transform thoughts into material objects. Whatever they desired they could produce, almost instantaneously, through these machines. They cultivated a huge underground laboratory containing virtually "infinite" sources of knowledge and energy. Morbius learned tremendously from these riches. He created a robot to do his bidding, and he worked tirelessly to attain their capabilities. Yet there was one point about which he remained perplexed: why did the Krell become extinct?

For several evenings in a row, Adams and his crew begin to be attacked by a strange immaterial force. It strikes without warning and steals raw materials from their ship. The crew sets up an electromagnetic fence around the ship in hopes of repelling the phenomenon. Later that evening, however, the force returns. It blasts into the fence and, as if fed by its energy, swells into a gigantic electromagnetic "beast." Although several men are vaporized by the assailant, it retreats, at least temporarily, in a blaze of ray-gun blasts.

Adams, meanwhile, redoubles his effort to understand the source of these attacks. Attended by his first officer, he demands a fuller explanation from Morbius. All Morbius can offer, however, is a sterner warning to leave. While the two argue, the first officer slips into the Krell lab and experiments with one of their mindstretching machines. The machine imparts invaluable knowledge to him, but at the same time racks and severely damages his brain. In the throes of death, he staggers over to Adams, and cries out: "Morbius . . . [came] close. But the Krell *completed* the project. That big machine, no instrumentalities, a true creation . . . but the Krell forgot one thing, monsters, John, monsters from the id!" Adams demands an explanation from Morbius, who explains that this is the outmoded term for our animal cravings, our base nature.

Suddenly, it dawns upon Adams—the illumination to the mystery of their plight: "The big machine . . . enough power for a whole population of creative geniuses, [is] operated by remote control, operated by the electromagnetic impulses of individual Krell brains." "To what purpose?" Morbius almost chidingly inquires. So that the "machine," Adams continues, "would instantaneously project solid matter to any part of the planet, in any shape or color that they might imagine. For *any* purpose, Morbius! Creation by mere thought." Adams goes on: "But like you the Krell forgot one deadly danger: their own subconscious hate and lust for destruction. . . . And so those mindless beasts of the subconscious had access to a machine that could *never* be shut down. The secret devil of every soul on the planet all set free at once to loot and maim, to take revenge, Morbius, and kill!"

Their present barbaric assailant, Adams goes on to explain, is itself a product of the subconscious. Moreover, that subconscious mind can belong to none other than Dr. Morbius himself, who—through Krell knowledge—also uses mental energy to affect the material world. But this energy is, at the same time, his downfall (as was true for the Krell), because only a portion of it is controllable. Although Morbius (like the Krell) could produce food, fuel, and technological wonders from this energy, he could not master its obscurer (subconscious) aims—aggressiveness, jealousy, the quest for power. Hence, it was this subconscious "monstrosity" that annihilated the Krell and that murdered Morbius's colleagues and rivals; and it is this same antagonist that threatens Adams and his crew. For the closer that Adams's crew comes to that which Morbius held dear (for example, Krell knowledge, the love of his daughter), the more they too court his unwitting antipathy.

"Something is approaching from the southwest," Morbius's robot presently declares, as Adams, Altaira, and Morbius cringe in desperation. Clear as to what this "something" is, Adams urges and convinces Morbius to "give up" his homicidal projections and his possessiveness of Altaira, of whom Adams is increasingly enamoured. The transformation, however, exacts a price. Deflecting his "evil side" from Adams and Altaira, he redirects it upon himself, destroying the guilty—though unwitting—agent.

In the final scene, Altaira, Adams, and the remainder of the crew depart from the planet. Adams turns to Altaira and muses: "Your father's light shall shine again—like a beacon into the galaxy. It will remind us that, after all, we are not God."

The encounters with space, with evolution, and with mental and physical boundaries are the leading thematic elements in *Forbidden Planet*. Although the film's production values and performances are somewhat dated, the *story* is both classic and prophetic. Elaborating upon many of the questions set forth by *Frankenstein* and *Dr. Jekyll and Mr. Hyde, Forbidden Planet* pursues the consequences of humanity's relentless quest for Godhood. Instead of gothic laboratories or gurgling test tubes, however, the setting here is astronautical, planetary, and electromagnetic. Human beings have become capable of far-reaching explorations, split-second technological operations, and vast intellectual feats. As the film so keenly demonstrates, however, they are juveniles when it comes to the fathomless perplexities of Being.

Forbidden Planet considers four issues that are simultaneously fascinating and horrifying: the transition from physical and tool-based adaptation to mental and energy-based creation; the idea of thought-creation—that anything we can conceive of or desire can be materialized; the issue of subconscious (or unwitting) influence; and the problem of limitless psychophysical power.

With *Forbidden Planet* (as with the more recent Stephen King narratives), we move from the glandular, creaturely excesses of our previously mentioned gothic tales to the further reaches of evolutionary possibility. Like Frankenstein, Morbius is a builder and a dreamer, but the resources at his command and the ambitiousness of his vision exceed the former's by a thousand-fold. With Krell knowledge at his disposal, Morbius unveils an electromagnetic wonderland. Tools, instruments, and bodily movement are decreasingly relevant in this world; only the mind and its capacity to conceive are essential. The Krell mindstretching technology has given Morbius the capability not just to observe but to control that wondrous intermingling of mind and matter, spirit and object that has confounded humanity for ages. One is staggered by the implications here—a human window on the measureless energies of space-time, consciousness, and the cosmos; a world of instantaneous travel, materialization and dematerialization. This is the cosmic playground with which Morbius tinkered.

Yet as with Frankenstein, Jekyll, Faust, and so many others in the pantheon of overreachers, so too Morbius loses his grip. The technology he utilizes is far too advanced for him—his brain fills it with too many signals; his desires direct it at too many targets; and his responsibility to manage the operation is taxed beyond calculation.

For as accomplished as science may one day become, *Forbidden Planet* warns, it will probably not eclipse the infinite. It will probably not foresee all the contingencies or account for all the blind spots. If we can actualize everything we imagine, for example, then along with comforts and conveniences, we must also actualize lust, greed, and the irrepressible quest for power. We must also actualize conflict among our fellows because human purposes are not always in agreement. Lastly, we must actualize the purposes of that which is unknown to or outside of us, and these may or may not be in proportion to our immediate intentions. The virtually limitless capacity of *Forbidden Planet's* subconscious "monstrosity" to self-generate, to feed on the energies mobilized to destroy it, is but one illustration of this point.

The moral of these scenarios, then, is cautionary: reach far into the universe, but at the same time be wary of *equating* ourselves with the universe.

This concludes our consideration of hyperexpansive horror. Although there are many such equivalents, *Dr. Jekyll and Mr. Hyde, The Birds,* and *Forbidden Planet* are three of the most astute: in *Jekyll* we explored the limits of physical power; in *The Birds* we examined our vulnerability to the natural terrors of living; and in *Forbidden Planet* we witnessed the ferocious potential of conscious and subconscious projection.

Whereas the hyperconstrictive tales discussed mapped out the boundaries of our withdrawal, these tales consider the boundaries of our emanation; whereas hyperconstrictive horror warned us about our ability to manage dissolution, hyperexpansive stories admonish us about our capacity to handle eruption. Irrespective of the case, however, it is the dialectic *between* the extremes that is fruitful and worthy of attainment.

James Stewart as Scottie Ferguson. From *Vertigo,* Paramount, 1958. Copyright © by Universal City Studios, Inc. Courtesy of MCA Publishing Rights, a division of MCA Inc.

84

Studies in Bipolar Horror

*For after all what is man in nature? A
nothing in regard to the infinite, a
whole in regard to nothing, a mean
between nothing and the whole; infinitely removed from understanding either extreme.*

—Blaise Pascal

To this point, we have concentrated on unipolar—
constrictive *or* expansive—horror. On the one hand, we have
peered into the splendrous, anxious worlds of nuance and detail,
and on the other, the marvelous yet monstrous realms of vastness
and disarray. Now, however, we will consider bipolar horror—
thrillers that not only *combine* but also *span* constrictive and
expansive motifs. First, we will consider Alfred Hitchcock's
masterwork, *Vertigo,* and second, Ridley Scott's *Alien.*

Vertigo *(1958 film version)*

*We burn with desire to find a steadfast
place and an ultimate fixed basis where-
on we may build a tower to reach the
infinite. But our whole foundation
breaks up, and earth opens to the
abysses.*

—Blaise Pascal

Vertigo is one of the richest motion pictures—let alone
suspense tales—ever made; I am not alone in this assessment
(Wood 1969). Plumbing our most prominent anxieties, which

are, at the same time, supreme desires, Hitchcock spans the polarities of our being.

Although *Vertigo* involves ghosts and monstrosities, they are much more *metaphorical* than in the previous stories we have discussed. The horrific core of the film, however, is completely consistent with those previous works. It concerns the deviation from (and ultimately contradiction of) conventional reality.

From the opening credits, we are shown graphic information about the film's central problem—vertigo—and the subjective perspective we shall be provided with on that problem. An alarmed, mysterious face emerges, the eyes of which move nervously from side to side. The camera zooms far into the iris of one of the eyes and spirals back out again to its point of origin. The effect of this scene suggests a sharp contrast. The tight, superficial perspective of the outer eye is compared with the depth, intensity, and bottomlessness of the inner eye (or of "reality" *behind* the appearance).

The opening scene of the story is no less metaphorical. A short metal bar is revealed against an obscure backdrop. Two hands suddenly clasp the bar, and a brightly lit city can be perceived behind and beneath them. Instantly, we understand the context of this shot: a man is clinging desperately to the side of a building and is deathly afraid of what is below him. A chase scene ensues in which this man is pursued by a policeman and a plainclothes detective. Suddenly, the detective himself loses his balance and latches onto a drain pipe. The drain pipe, however, begins cracking and the detective is left hanging in the air. His colleague (the other officer) returns to try to save him but in the process also slips and tumbles to his death on the street below. The camera converges again on the desperately clinging detective. His movements are delicate, restrained. This narrow perspective, however, is soon coupled with a breathtaking swoop of the depths below. The detective is aghast but also strangely entranced by his predicament.

The detective, we discover, is a San Francisco police veteran named Scottie Ferguson. He has just stumbled while pursuing a suspect but somehow managed to escape major physical injury.

The scene accelerates into the future, and Scottie is safely seated in his girlfriend Midge's apartment. Midge is conventional and predictable. Her apartment is pleasant but somewhat sterile. As the camera pans to Scottie, it is clear that he is unsettled. He tries balancing the cane he acquired for a broken leg, but it falls to the ground. He speaks about how the corset he wears "binds" him and how much he looks forward to being a "free man" the next day when it is to come off. But just as he contemplates the prospect, he bristles from the pain.

"Do you know many men who wear corsets?" he asks Midge rhetorically.

Scottie had had ambitions to become chief of police, we find out, but because of his fall developed a disabling form of acrophobia (or fear of heights) and the vertigo (or dizziness) which attends that condition. Midge tries to pacify him by urging him to accept a "desk job." "Don't be so *motherly,*" he snaps back. Later in the scene, Scottie is intrigued by a bra Midge has on display. She is a draftsperson of some sort and has been sketching the bra's construction: "works on the principle of the cantilever bridge," she dryly and incongruously notes. "An aircraft engineer down on the Peninsula designed it."

At every turn now, Scottie is confronted by his dilemma. He is alive but "trapped" in the apartment of (and in his relationship with) his pedestrian girlfriend (even the name "Midge" is suggestive of suppression). He was strong and brave once, but now he is an impotent hobbler. He longs for freedom, but he is dragged down by mundaneness, resignation, and guilt (for his inability to help the officer). He longs to expand and enrich his life, and beyond that, to be superhuman if possible, to undo the tragedy which befell him.

Later in the scene, Scottie develops a theory that he believes will help him overcome his vertigo. By confronting his fear in steps, with the use of an adjustable chair, he hopes to work through his dilemma. Although a viable solution, as we shall suggest later on, Scottie is so desperate to compensate for his phobia that he turns arrogant and overreaches himself. "There's nothin' to it," he quips, as he brusquely elevates himself above Midge's picture window. With one sweeping gaze at the streets below, however, Scottie buckles—both entranced and horrified by the scene before him.

Back and forth we swing, between stability and turbulence, clarity and obscurity. The smoothness and evenness of conventional reality is contrasted with the jagged, spiraling world of "freedom," "power," and death. By juxtaposing and interchanging these worlds, Hitchcock suggests the ever-present availability of transcendent realms. If only we really looked, he hints, we would see. If only we took the plunge, as Scottie moves closer to doing, we would understand. And yet, do we (or Scottie) truly *want* to understand, Hitchcock questions? Are we *willing* to confront the consequences?

In the next scene, Scottie emphatically replies to this query. After meeting with a shipping magnate and former college friend named Elster, he agrees to an intriguing request: to monitor and investigate the movements of Elster's puzzling wife, Madeline. Her incomprehensibility, we are informed, refers to her perception of being possessed and marked for death. Although Scottie is skeptical of what *he*, as opposed to a psychologist, can do to help her, something compels him to find out.

Madeline, Scottie soon discovers, is an extraordinary woman. She is obsessed with the past and evokes an otherworldly, timeless quality. Like an angelic ghost, she meanders from place to place, time to time. She exudes a grace and a mystery that completely defy contemporary fashion. Far from the business offices, far from the hard, encrusted surfaces of modern living, Madeline leads Scottie on a procession of dream-like adventures. She wanders to a lake, then a graveyard, then a museum. She spends an afternoon at the former home of a dead Spanish noblewoman. Scottie wanders with her and the more he observes, the more deeply he is transfixed. For he too longs to escape (transcend?) the world of routine and banality and drift toward the beatific. Madeline's obsessions, then, soon become his own, and he spirals ever more deeply into her universe.

When Scottie finally meets Madeline, it is against a background of desperation and romance. Observing her plunge into the San Francisco Bay in an apparent suicide attempt, he springs into the water and rescues her. The mist from the crashing waves rises wildly as he carries her ashore. Holding Madeline in his arms, he ascends the cliffs overlooking the bay and becomes a part of one of the most dazzling spectacles in cinema history.

The more Scottie becomes involved with Madeline, the less sure we become about her mortality. She is bathed in dream-like imagery and Scottie, like Hitchcock's camera, is awhirl in her sensuality, dazzled by her precariousness.

Each scene is significant in this film, each a reflection of and elaboration upon the whole. At a visit to the Sequoia forest, Scottie and Madeline examine the rings of a felled tree. "Somewhere here I was born," Madeline mutters, as she points hypnotically at one of the rings. "There I died," she declares. Again she is preoccupied with the past, the spiraling core, the eternal. And again Hitchcock attends to the winding depths of our perception—in this case, the dizzying composition of the rings.

Moments later, Madeline vanishes, as she had vanished and reappeared so many times before. Scottie is alarmed but undeterred. He seeks her out and discovers her behind a tree.

Madeline takes several trips to a museum and sits in front of a painting of the Spanish noblewoman Carlotta Valdes, a woman of whom she believes that she is the reincarnation. She positions herself in front of the painting for hours, and again, Scottie tracks her, fixating on her every move. Ever prepared for the symbolic, Hitchcock leads our eye directly into the spiraling strands of Madeline's hairbun.

Convinced that she must follow in the same, ultimately fatal, footsteps as those of Carlotta, Madeline drives out to an old bell tower at San Juan Baptista mission. With Scottie in hot pursuit, she ascends the staircase (which is of course, a *winding* one) to the very top. Although he is determined to stop her, Scottie's vertigo effectively immobilizes him. The next thing he observes (from halfway up the stairs) is what appears to be Madeline's body plunging fatally to the roof below.

Scottie is devastated by Madeline's apparent suicide and begins a long descent into depression. A hearing is conducted, in which he is roundly condemned for negligence. He ends up in a sanitarium for awhile, but it seems that he is beyond help, at least that which can be offered either by psychiatrists or by his girlfriend Midge.

A broken man, Scottie departs from the psychiatric clinic and sets out to reclaim his life. The specter of Madeline, however, exercises an unrelenting influence over him. A woman turns around, and for an instant, he believes, she is Madeline. A thought, a sensation, an image, each can trigger her aura. His dreams too are filled by associations with her. In one dream, a posy that Madeline had plucked apart just before her suicide explodes in dramatic, cartoon-like fashion. The next dream-image shows Scottie, Elster, and Carlotta Valdes poised between them. In the final sequence, Scottie walks toward and plunges directly into Carlotta's open grave. He descends as though in a bottomless pit. This image dissolves into that of a man falling directly onto a roof (just as Madeline had apparently done). The roof disintegrates and the man continues to fall, hurtling endlessly into space.

This scene suggests that Scottie's identification with Madeline (or the ideal that she symbolizes) is complete (Wood 1969). He passionately embraces her eternal image—if only in his dream—and is mesmerized by its power.

A short time later, he meets Judy, a rather crude, vampish woman who bears a striking resemblance to Madeline. He takes great pains to court Judy and to revive in her the radiant splendor of Madeline. Working feverishly, desperately, he dresses her in Madeline's style of clothing and supervises her make-up. Although Judy reluctantly plays along with his scheme, she soon reveals to him an astonishing complication: she *is* Madeline, or rather, the Madeline that Scottie knew. Elster had employed her in an intricate plot to murder his wife. He hired her, it turns out, to play the role of his wife (Madeline) so that Scottie, whom Elster knew suffered from vertigo, could be lured to the scene of the crime. When Judy (in the role of Madeline) reached the top of the bell-tower, Elster pushed the real Madeline off the tower, leaving Scottie both dumbfounded and responsible (in part) for her death.

With these discoveries, Scottie compels Judy, now dressed as Madeline, to return to the scene of the murder. Partly out of spite, partly to confront his vertigo, he badgers her to accompany him up the winding staircase. When they reach the top, Scottie presses Madeline against the open window. He forces her to look down, to gaze into the full brunt of her responsibility. Moments later, a black figure (which turns out to be a nun) emerges from the stairwell. Petrified by her initial impression of this figure, Madeline slips backwards and plunges onto that same roof that Elster's wife had crashed upon months earlier.

The film ends with Scottie peering into the great depths

where Judy lies lifeless. He has overcome his vertigo, it is clear. But at the same time, he has renounced his claim on the eternal. He is more functional, perhaps, but thoroughly stripped of the dream that Madeline had represented to him.

The greatness of *Vertigo* lies in its grasp of the human condition. We are all plagued by life's routines. We are all lured by a larger reality. The question is, how are we to handle this conflict, and what will be the consequences of our struggle?

Scottie chooses not only to follow but to plunge into his dreams. He throws himself into the transcendent (symbolized by his vertigo) in search of a rejuvenated sense of self. He is anxious about this path, yet even more repulsed by the prospect of a conventional life with Midge. But Scottie is naive about the scope of his project. He is only partially aware of its complexity.

The further he looks into this complexity, the more his mind is awhirl. He spirals into the world of secrecy and the ethereal (as evinced, for example, by Madeline's mysteriousness and the graceful way that she moves). We follow him into Madeline's covert world: her disappearance and sudden reemergence, her flirtation with ghosts and the historical, and her trance-like gravitation toward death. Scottie is engulfed by this all-consuming world, disintegrating, racing toward final surrender.

Scottie spirals out, on the other hand, into dizzying emotional and physical highs. He learns love and lust and all-consuming passion. He abandons duties, schedules, and plans, and in their stead courts spontaneity, unpredictability, and surprise. He merges with Madeline and strides gleefully into her dramas.

Yet as Hitchcock and so many other chroniclers of the macabre have shown, Scottie (and those of his ilk) spin tragically out of control. They are so intent on having it *all* that they squander that which it is possible to attain. They believe that they have only two choices: to capitulate to the oppressive order, or to leap headlong into cosmic bliss. Yet there is a third way, these writers imply. This is the way of inquiry, deliberation, and elasticity.

For example, if Scottie could have seen Madeline (or more properly, Judy) for the woman that she was, he might have saved himself a great deal of grief. A more mature man probably would not have wasted his energy on her; or if he had become involved

with her, he would have anticipated (and perhaps helped her work through) her shortcomings.

Scottie, on the other hand, overreached and crashed. He fell in love not merely with Madeline but with the fathomless depths of consciousness. These depths could not be spanned, and so understandably, inevitably, he recoiled from them. His withdrawal was symbolized by his inability to climb the bell tower in the first half of the film and by his recognition, ultimately, that Judy was not Madeline, but deceitful, conniving, and soberingly mortal. Scottie's crash landing, then, his return to the world of security and explanation, nullified his vertigo. But it also dampened his wonder. He became *grounded,* but uninspired, *steadied,* but devitalized. "If you take away my demons," Scottie could now cry with Rilke, "will my angels be far behind?"

And yet there *is* a possibility of transformation in *Vertigo.* One can feel it in the final scene, as Scottie peers into the fatal depths. Will he return to the oppressive social order, or will he preserve his flirtation with the fantastic? Will he destroy himself, or will he savor his earthly lot? Hitchcock does not say.

Alien *(1979 film version)*

Is it that by its indefiniteness it shadows forth the heartless voids and immensities of the universe, and thus stabs us from behind with the thought of annihilation . . . ?

—HERMAN MELVILLE

Ridley Scott's *Alien* is one of the most compelling tales of *terror* of which I am aware. I emphasize the term "terror" here, because of the film's literal rather than symbolic confrontation with infinitude. The terror of *Alien,* however, is so gripping, so utterly disarming, that it forces us to entertain one persistent question throughout: how does the film achieve these effects? We will consider this issue momentarily.

Alien opens with long tracking shots of a spaceship corridor. The languishing quality of the scene, as the camera wends its way through a variety of metallic hallways, is suggestive of the formidable perils ahead. The ship, a cargo carrier called *Nostromo* (named after the 1904 Joseph Conrad novel, *Nostromo*?), is eleven months from earth. The crew of Nostromo are a rather crude, exasperated bunch. They have just completed their mission and are wearily returning to earth. Suddenly, they receive a curious distress call from a nearby planet. At first, the crew balks at the idea of responding to the call, but the first officer, Captain Dallas, feels obliged and challenged to investigate.

Reluctantly, the crew guides the ship into the dark, dank, haze that is the planet's atmosphere. It is "primordial," the science officer, Ash, quips. An investigative team is sent to the source of the distress signal. Gradually, anxiously, we accompany the team into the forbidding recesses of their destination. As the team enters what appears to be a gigantic cavern, one member, Kane, detects and runs his hand through a clear, repellent ooze. Undaunted by his discovery, Kane steps into what appears to be a riverbed of sorts. He stoops down and touches one of the egg-like structures dotting the riverbed. Ash, meanwhile, pleads with Kane to return to the ship, but Kane seems fixated, almost mesmerized, by his investigation. Suddenly, and with lightning bolt force, a multi-legged organism springs out of an egg and splats onto Kane's helmet.

The rest of the team manages to bring Kane back to the ship, but the strong, ethically-minded second officer, Ripley, will not let them aboard. Despite Dallas's orders to the contrary, she is concerned that bringing him and the entity aboard constitutes an unacceptable risk for the entire crew. Science Officer Ash, however, appears to be oblivious to this risk and brazenly grants the team entry. Hastily, Kane is placed on an examining table while Dallas and Ash consider his condition. Kane is alive, they find, but in the grip of a large multi-tendrilled creature on his head. X-rays show that the creature has penetrated his body with a long cylindrical tube. Bewildered by the intricacy of their task, the officers attempt to cut the being's tentacle as a step toward removing its entire body from the victim's head. The moment they proceed, however, the being's internal fluid—a highly corrosive substance—splatters onto and burns its way through the examining room floor. Failing to stop there, the fluid continues to melt through several lower landings, until it ceases, at the very *bottom* of the ship's hull!

Perplexed and exasperated, Kane and his unwelcome "guest" are left alone for a period of time. Several days later, Ash reports a change in Kane's condition: the parasite appears to have expired, and Kane has been freed from its grip. Kane and the crew celebrate this hopeful turn with a dinner party. Halfway through the meal, however, Kane turns extraordinarily pallid. He begins to choke, and with a violent paroxysm of pain hurls himself onto the dining table. Terror-stricken, the crew holds Kane down. Yet he is irrepressible and successfully knocks them and surrounding objects away. Flailing about with no apparent cause, Kane's chest begins to protrude. In the next scene, one of the most nauseating images we are ever likely to see ensues: the alien, in a slightly more mature form following its brief period of gestation or pupation, bursts out of Kane's chest and vanishes into the recesses of the ship.

The rest of the film pits the entity—continually increasing in size as well as craftiness—against a crew of rapidly diminishing number. One by one they attempt to rid themselves of the beast, and one by one they are devoured by it. A crucial point arises when we discover that Ash is actually a robot and has all along been on a mission to capture and ensure the safe return of the alien to earth. His "mission," it appears, was sponsored by a group of naive and unscrupulous scientists who had hoped to study the being. Upon learning that the robot considers the rest of the crew "expendable," the remaining crewmembers subdue him. Before they destroy him, however, they inquire about his knowledge of the alien. "I admire its purity," he declares, "a survivor, unclouded by conscience, remorse, or delusions of morality." With regard to their chances of terminating the creature, the robotic officer replies: "you have my sympathies."

The climactic ending of the story involves second officer Ripley. As the sole survivor, she must battle with the creature even as she appears to escape the mothership in a shuttlecraft. Finally, she is able to blast the creature into outer space. The question as to its demise, however, is cleverly left unanswered.

As the title of the film implies, the encounter with otherness, with radical deviation, is *Alien*'s prime thematic focus. What it lacks in symbolic richness, *Alien* makes up for in its sweeping capacity to disarm. It is a paragon of terror.

The alien world upon which we descend is both remote and blurringly close. It is quite different from what we or the crew are accustomed to, and yet it looms undeniably before us. Everywhere we look, obstruction and obfuscation abound—blinding haze, acidic downpour, coiled and bulbous shapes, immense cavernous hulls. Everything about this planet is inhospitable and yet perversely, provocatively inviting.

The investigative team staggers through the alien terrain and confidently enters into one of the cavernous chambers. We cannot help, at this point, but be impressed by the sheer immensity of the team's surroundings—its many convolutions and mammoth openings. Is it alive, or is it inanimate? we wonder; is it autonomous, or is it rooted in the hard, wet terrain of the planet? Or is it an elaborate byproduct of some larger beast, which has yet to emerge from its lair? Like a drawing by Bosch, the possibilities and puzzlements appear hopelessly intertwined.

At the same time that we are struck by the object's awesome size, its inaccessibility is equally baffling. Somewhere within the repulsive ooze that it emits, somewhere beneath the murky riverbed in which it is ensconced, something unsettling remotely lurks.

The remaining portions of the film draw out both the ineptitude and understandable preoccupations of the crew involved. Their understandable curiosity about and pursuit of the alien is exemplified by Ash's remark about its purity—the creature embodies the qualities of Dracula and Frankenstein's monster rolled up into one. The alien has a tremendous capacity, for example, not just for survival but for virtual invincibility. It is explosive, lightning-swift, brutally deceptive and cunning. It can live in both animate and inanimate domains and unabashedly consumes the energy of that with which it comes into contact.

Inasmuch as it is an object of ceaseless fascination, however, it is also one of incalculable danger. The very traits that make it astonishing—especially from a scientific point of view—also make it unbearable, far beyond the human capacity to subsume. We simply cannot handle its range, speed, and elusiveness; and these recall the very contractions and dilations of the cosmos itself.

Curiosity, then, applied indiscriminately, led to the demise of the *Nostromo,* and few aboard (such as Ripley) seemed capable of apprehending this problem. Kane, the victimized officer at the start of the film, for example, prodded clumsily and ultimately fatally among the aliens' eggs. Science officer Ash and Captain Dallas imprudently ignored the need for basic decontamination procedures. A group of selfish, morally bankrupt scientists, finally, attempted to return the alien to earth for research purposes. Yet the alien, as Ripley anticipated, was not to be toyed with. It was neither a harmless "specimen" for scientific analysis nor a candidate for domestication; it was a dynamic, life-threatening being, a *humbling* product of nature.

Vertigo and *Alien* each exhibit the human dreads of constrictive and expansive infinitude. In *Vertigo* we spin into the utmost reaches of consciousness, encompassing at one moment, surrendering in the next. We are catapulted by this film into joy, ecstasy, and cosmic mergence; and we are swallowed up by whispers, subtle seductions, and specters from the past. In *Alien* it is a devouring beast on a small ship in the infinity of space that excites our fears. Both explosive and hidden, engulfing and imperceptible, the being simultaneously stretches and squeezes consciousness.

For all their convulsing drama, however, *Alien* and *Vertigo,* as with the previous works we have discussed, do have a redemptive message: our course lies somewhere *between* fanaticism and despair.

This concludes the section on wisdom-horror. We next turn to the implications of our tales for contemporary living. What lessons do they hold for us as individuals and societies? What do they imply about psychiatric problems, substance abuse, and psychological well-being? What morals do they imply for science, religion, and politics? In short, what light can classic horror shed on humanity's core dilemma—the tension between our freedom and our limits?

The Crest of Niagara Falls (1968). Photo by Algimantas Kezys.

Part IV
Horror as a Worldview

It is dangerous to prove to man too plainly how nearly he is on a level with the brutes without showing him his greatness; it is also dangerous to show him his greatness too clearly apart from his vileness. It is still more dangerous to leave him in ignorance of both. But it is of great advantage to show him both.

—Blaise Pascal

As I gaze about my cluttered office in the early months of 1991, I realize that my heart is burdened. Halfway around the world, thunderous bombing raids are being carried out. A new war, an ancient form of "conflict resolution," is leaving its mark. They say that the cause is just but I have other sentiments.[1]

As I return to my little cubicle, my laboratory of reflection, I consider that the lessons of classic horror continue to go unheeded. I consider that, in so many ways, on so many fronts, human existence has oscillated between two essential tendencies —fanaticism and despair. On the one hand, we are hasty to take up a cause or direction. We pursue it without pause; we become intoxicated by our desires. On the other hand, we feel resigned. We can neither imagine nor innovate, question nor fight; we feel sapped, spent, and immobilized by change. The upshot of these reactions is that the hasty become emotional and physical wrecks, and the desperate bathe quietly in their misery.

Classic horror can serve as an instructive metaphor for these dilemmas. Whether it is the maniacal rage sported by Mr. Hyde or the maleficent control practiced by Dracula, whether we are electrified or appalled, classic horror challenges us to mediate our reactions. It beckons us to approach otherness, extravagance, and the like mindful of *both* limits and possibilities. It calls on us neither to recoil in dread nor to leap with wantonness but to stop, pause, and reflect deeply upon the phenomenon before us. The question that horror poses is, what is it about this phenomenon that both attracts and repels; how can we learn from it and fruitfully integrate it into our lives?

Classic horror, therefore, underscores the virtue of paradox. It teaches us that human potentiality (amazement, excitement, freedom) is the flipside of human anxiety (revulsion, disgust, discomfort) and that *both* are essential for wisdom. Sacrifice either one or cultivate either one to the exclusion of the other and, as we have so often witnessed in this book, you breed individual, social, and environmental catastrophe.

To sum up, then, classic horror maneuvers *between* fanaticism and despair. It points to a third, and in many ways, revolutionary path for humanity—the way I call "wonderment."[2]

Between Fanaticism and Despair:
Toward a Worldview of Wonderment

Yet who shall declare the dark theme a
positive handicap? Radiant with beau-
ty, the Cup of the Ptolemies was carven
of onyx.

—H.P. LOVECRAFT

For the purposes of this study, wonderment combines the idea of inquiry ("to wonder about") with enchantment ("to wonder at"). It means neither to fanatically worship nor to lethargically resign from a cause or object, but to be curious about, interested in, and searching toward the cause or object. While wonderment transcends the paralysis of despair, it simultaneously recognizes the cautionary value of that state; and while it rebukes fanaticism, it also concurrently acknowledges the dynamism of that condition. Wonderment is thus a form of *suspense* whereby one can be both appreciative of and vigilant toward the world around one.

While wonderment celebrates mystery, it does not countenance indecision. By contrast, wonderment is a basis for decision-making and fortifies decision-making with thoughtfulness, sensitivity, and flexibility. To be sure, wonderment can be abused. One might be tempted to indulge in the experience at ill-advised moments, such as when one's life is immediately threatened or when sharp analytical skills are called for. But by and large wonderment enriches (rather than weakens) the decision-making process. The attitude itself, moreover, serves as a check against prospective abuse. Rabid enthusiasm, for example, is accompanied (more or less) by commensurate skepticism; immoderate suspicion, likewise, is attended by proportionate fascination. Fanaticism and despair, by contrast, resist such counterbalances.

Let us now look more closely at the attitude of wonderment. In particular, let us consider wonderment and its interplay with fanaticism and despair in three crucial areas of life—psychology, science, and religion.

Wonderment in Psychology

The question is not yet settled whether madness is or is not the loftiest intelligence—whether much that is glorious—whether all that is profound —does not spring from disease of thought. . . .

—EDGAR ALLAN POE

Wonderment helps to explain one of the chief riddles of human behavior: the marvelous in madness and the maddening in the marvelous. What, for example, draws us to dark, seedy places, vulgar crowds, or violent contests? What intrigues us about deformed people, exotic insects, or ferocious animals? Why do we flock to mudbaths or fixate on menacing billow of fire? What compels us about auto accidents or hateful depictions of war?

Stated even more baldly, what titillates us about punishing another person or watching someone writhe in pain? Why do cheating, lying, and stealing stimulate us, or recklessness thrill us?

On the other hand, why is radiant beauty so *alarming*? What is it about a ravishing man or woman that shocks us? What makes us tremble before mountains, monuments, or sparkling palaces? What haunts us in glistening forests or opulent cities? Why do power, strength, and genius pulverize us?

We are now ready to deliberate upon these puzzlements.

The Marvelous in Madness

Our study of classic horror leads us to a rather startling conclusion: madness, agony, ugliness, and the like are not simply bleak or negative dimensions; they are not simply the dark sides of an otherwise immaculate existence. For all of their justified repulsiveness, by contrast, they can also serve congenial, even exultant, functions; they can serve as gateways to entirely fresh realms of perceiving.

This, I believe, is what Rilke (1982, p. 266) meant in his letter to a melancholic poet: "Were it possible to see further than our knowledge reaches . . . perhaps we would endure our sadnesses with greater confidence than our joys. For they are the moments when something new has entered us, something unknown." Nietzsche (1872/1956, p. 124) may have had a similar idea in mind when he wrote: "Dare to lead the life of the tragic man and you will be redeemed."

The so-called prurient interest in the unsavory, then, may not be entirely due to some brain defect or poor upbringing, but an honest curiosity. The gawker at freak shows or car accidents, the gazer at violence or the grotesque, even the sneak, thief, or aggressor may not *invariably* harbor malicious motives. Note that I stress "invariably" here, for in relative degrees their motives are sometimes untoward. But my point is that all of us, at one time or another, can identify with such individuals, and it would be a high miscalculation to wholly pathologize them or us.

The upshot of this discussion is that the unsavory captivates us. In some basic, bodily way, we are entranced by it. What element of the repulsive accomplishes this task? Once again, we are struck by the role played by deviation, contradiction, and ultimately constrictive and expansive infinitude. When bodies are hacked up, when blood is spurting, when beings are growling, when people are copulating, or battling, or deceiving— these are disturbing developments. But they are at the same time *amazing* developments. For like the crashing of waves, changing of seasons, or eruption of mountains, they evoke the very rhythms of life.[3]

Given the unsavory's salutary aspects, does this not provide at least a hint of solace to those in distress? Does it not yield a flicker of possibility to those whom we term neurotic or psychotic? That this, indeed, is the case is attested to by a sizable number of clinical studies (see for example Buckley 1981; Grof and Grof 1989; Kaplan 1964; Laing 1967; Lukoff 1988; and Richards 1981). Similarly, classic horror implies that depression, dependency, obsession, mania, and other psychiatric "syndromes" are *different* (not necessarily inferior) dimensions of experience. When those afflicted with such conditions are encouraged to consider the privileged (as well as indisputably painful) aspects of their perspectives, they often acquire a renewed sense of themselves. This is also the message of classic horror: if the monster learns appropriate restraint, it becomes an angel. Dracula, for example, could have become a celebrated psychologist. By "reading" his patients' thoughts and communicating telepathically, he could have liberated hundreds of anguished souls. He could have become a renowned physicist, penetrating the deepest recesses of the atom or electrical energy. He could have brilliantly disclosed the animating properties of human blood, or he could have become a poet, attuning himself to the most delicate nuances of romantic love.

In some forms of *psychiatric* constriction we find corresponding possibilities. The slowness and oppressiveness of depression, for example, are legendary. Volumes have been written about its isolating, stupefying effects. For those who can look on the malady in retrospect, on the other hand, moments of concrete realization are also not unheard of. Depression, for example, can strip away people's cheerful (but contrived) facades. It can help them to unveil hidden values, talents, and needs. The quietude that depression provides can foster productive self-exploration and even innovation. It can convey to people a great deal about their own limitations and about the resources or friends that they formerly took for granted. Depression, in short, is a retreat of some sort; it is a release from the conventional world of haste and a chance to reassess as well as recede.

William Styron (1990) writes soberly:

> For those who have dwelt in depression's dark wood, their return from the abyss is not unlike the ascent of the poet, trudging upward and upward out of hell's black depths and at last emerging into what he saw as the "shining world." There, whoever has been restored to health has almost always been restored to the capacity for serenity and joy . . .(p. 84).

Obsessive-compulsiveness is also an edifying dysfunction. Like the Phantom of the Opera, the obsessive-compulsive has a great capacity for craftiness. He or she can attend to the tiniest detail or map out the most intricate strategy. The Phantom, thus, might have become a master composer, architect, or engineer. He could have served city planners and stupendous orchestras. He might have even served the police with his uncanny knowledge of guile. The Shrinking Man, the Invisible Man, Roderick Usher, and many other oddities of hyperconstrictive horror might also display these talents. They are all explorers and specialists in the miniature. They hear and see what we cannot or will not explore, and they investigate the hidden wisdom of history, although too often they are victims of what their experience reveals. As Shapiro (1965) writes about his obsessive-compulsive patients, the very "same qualities that make these people seem so rigid in one context endow them, in another, with excellent technical facility and an impressive capacity for concentration . . ." (p. 30).

The intemperances of hyperexpansion, likewise, are also potentially instructive. Hyde's histrionics, for example, could have been enlivening in one not quite so reckless; he could have become a feisty politician or inspiring actor. Frankenstein's grandiosity could have served visionary rather than indulgent aims; he could have revolutionized medicine and advanced human adaptation. Once harnessed, the manic energy of Dr. Morbius could have led to undreamed-of technological innovations—intergalactic travel, vast individual and social reforms. Scottie Ferguson's frenzied passion (in *Vertigo*) could have been applied to rich and creative spiritual commitments, both alone and with a more attainable partner. I am reminded here of the words of a manic patient in the early phase of his disorder: "from the first the experience seemed to me to be holy. What I saw was the Power of Love—the name that came to me at once—the power that I knew somehow to have made all universes, past, present, and to come . . ." (Custance, quoted in Kaplan 1964, p. 50).

In the most extreme forms of constrictive and expansive dysfunction, we witness an even mightier element of fascination. Schizophrenia, or what Laing (1969, p. 163) terms the "catatonic-hebephrenic" axis, is a case in point. Schizophrenia highlights, above all, the magnitude of human perception—seemingly endless withdrawls and fragmentations, and yet at the same time, explosions and engulfments. Some of the most compelling treatises on this condition are included in a book by

Bert Kaplan (1964) called *The Inner World of Mental Illness*. Here, psychiatric patients detail their "universe[s] of horror," as one inmate put it, and rival anything uttered by Shelley. Lara Jefferson, for example, sketched the following about a neighboring patient:

> She lies there in silence and hatred . . . There is a black pall of madness; brooding, waiting—and watching. It emanates from her and settles around her in sinister foreboding silence.
>
> To feel her eyes sweep you is to feel a chillness blown from caverns of hatred, black, vast and bottomless. To meet her eyes squarely is to feel something within you turn away quickly, chilled with the knowledge that it has seen naked madness—heavy, pregnant with horror unborn. (p. 20)

Jefferson's observation of another patient stresses that rapture, too, is an element in these torments.

> To see such a creature as she is stand naked—and howling with madness, is to wonder whether or not she is real; or an illusion both grim and lovely. It does not seem possible that life could be such a grim sculptor as to carve from smooth, living beauty the exquisite details of a cameo, then set such lovely perfection in a mounting of madness. (pp. 20–21)

Jefferson concludes about madness in general that,

> No phenomenon of nature is so awe inspiring. A typhoon—a Niagara or the ebb and flow of oceans can be caught and held in harness as easily as a deranged mind! Nothing will stay it—there is nothing that can hold it; nothing with the power to deter it when it sweeps out to pursue its destiny through the dim caverns of itself. (p. 32)

The awe-filled features of madness—as with horror—are illustrated further by this "anonymous" patient:

> Shortly after I was taken to the hospital . . . in a rigid catatonic condition, I was plunged into the horror of a world of catastrophe. I was being caught up in a cataclysm and totally dislocated. . . . Part of the time I was exploring a new planet (a marvelous and breathtaking adventure) but it was too lonely, I could persuade no one to settle there, and I had to get back to earth somehow. The earth, however, had been devastated by atomic bombs and most of its inhabitants killed. Only a few

people—myself and the dimly perceived nursing staff—had escaped. . . .

The issue of world salvation was of predominant importance and I was trying to tell people how to go back to the abandoned earth. All personal matters relating to my family were forgotten. At times when the universe was collapsing, I was not sure that things would turn out all right. I thought I might have to stay in the endless hell-fire of atomic destruction. (p. 95)

The passage concludes with the most riveting consternation of all: "The chief horror consisted in the fact that I would never be able to die" (p. 95).

One of the most exhilarating descriptions of psychosis is provided by Jesse Watkins:

I had a feeling at times of an enormous journey . . . a fantastic journey, and I had got an understanding of things which I'd been trying to understand for a long time, problems of good and evil and so on. . . . I had come to the conclusion . . . that I was more—more than I had always imagined myself. . . . [A]head of me was lying the most horrific journey . . . a journey to . . . the final sort of business of . . . being aware of all—everything . . . and I felt this so strongly, it was such a horrifying experience to suddenly feel . . . that I immediately shut myself off from it because I couldn't contemplate it. . . . (quoted in Laing 1967, pp. 154–55)

It should be evident by now that it is *infinitude* that draws us to the unsavory; *infinitude* that lurks behind dread. The eccentric, the altered, and the deranged are but amplified marvels, enticing and yet dismaying in their implications.

We have already considered the enticing aspects of these extravagances—sensitivity, craftiness, and vitality; but what of the dismaying aspects? What, for example, *discourages* Dracula from tempering his occultism, or *diverts* Frankenstein from limiting his scientific aspirations? What *impedes* psychiatric patients from constructively utilizing their powers? While the answer to these questions is complex, the relationship between wonderment and fanaticism is surely at its heart.

Classic horror informs us that the dividing line between wonderment (the enticing side of madness) and fanaticism (the dismaying side) is one of control: those who stand in wonder, for example, exercise some degree of choice over their perceptions. They are motivated less by defensiveness and more by affirmation, less by absolutism and more by curiosity. To illustrate this point, we need only think of the zeal and yet appropriate reserve of Abraham Van Helsing. The fanatic, on the other hand, entirely lacks such counterbalances. Motivated by need, compulsion, and dread, the fanatic becomes extreme, ironically, to avoid an extreme, to become *immune*. The tragedy, of course, is that far from being removed from danger, the fanatic plunges, pell-mell, into a reverse but equivalent peril. Dracula's vendetta against his ancient enemies, for example, led to his occultism; Frankenstein's monster's resentment of social ostracism instigated his rage; the Phantom's sense of rejection, likewise, inspired his life of trickery; the Invisible Man's feelings of inferiority activated his sadism; the Usher family's eccentricities were associated with their "collapse"; Hyde's reaction to Jekyll's prudishness motivated his anarchy; the Alien's revulsion to outsiders contributed to its ruthlessness; Scottie's defense against monotony spurred his delirium; and so on.

The fanatic reactions of many who become dysfunctional parallel the foregoing. This is illustrated by the depressive who is traumatized by assertiveness, the obsessive who is petrified by unruliness, or the manic who is deathly afraid of melancholy (see Schneider 1990).

The fascination with madness, then, is understandable, desirable, and in some cases highly laudable. A treasure trove of possibility awaits the explorer of such "deviations." But there is an equally important dimension that must be considered. This is the dimension of drivenness. It is the dimension of National Socialism, for example, in which all power becomes focalized on the racial mythology.[4] It is the dimension of intoxication, mob justice, and the vast array of fundamentalisms. It is the dimension, finally, that separates the interested from the addicted, the enchanted from the rabid, and the creative from the monstrous.

The Maddening in the Marvelous

At the same time as there is a luster in madness, there is a comparable madness in luster. Not only do a parade of in-patients attest to this observation (by, for example, their maniacal glee), but so also do a procession of historical geniuses.

What, we may ask, could be so *dismaying* about that which ostensibly is enthralling? What could alarm us about wealth, success, and power, or immobilize us before beauty? What makes Frankenstein's romantic rescuer, Walton, so *disturbing*, or the elegant Madeline so *appalling*?

The fact is that genius, beauty, power, and the like *are* unsettling. They upset the familiar order. Think, for example, about the myriad ways we try to avoid such intensities. How often we evade the eyes of attractive people, forego high-brow gatherings or demanding tasks, find the *easiest* relationship, the most *convenient* lifestyle—all to steer shy of bedazzlement.

After many years of studying such processes, Abraham Maslow arrived at a similar conclusion. Many of us are afraid of stretching ourselves, he suggested. We cringe before our own and others' greatness. Elsewhere he elaborates:

> We fear our highest possibilities, (as well as our lowest ones). We are generally afraid to become that which we can glimpse in our most perfect moments . . . We enjoy and even thrill to the godlike possibilities we see in ourselves in such peak moments. And yet we simultaneously shiver with weakness, awe, and fear before these very same possibilities (Maslow 1967, p. 163).

Granting the *dysfunctional* aspects of this pattern, which Maslow terms "the Jonah syndrome," he also reminds us of its *adaptive* value. There are sometimes good reasons to quiver, he notes. "So often, people in . . . ecstatic moments say, 'it's too much,' or 'I can't stand it,' or 'I could die.' . . . Delirious happiness cannot be borne for long. Our organisms are just too weak for any large doses of greatness" (p. 165).

Although other investigators have expressed similar sentiments (for example, May 1985, Otto 1958), the work of Martin Buber is of particular interest in the light of our thesis. Our fear of greatness, Buber relates, is not a fear of success or excitement *per se* but a dread of their ultimate implications—unbearability, vastness, groundlessness. "Once the concept of infinity [is] taken seriously," Buber elaborates (1965), "a human dwelling can no longer be made of the universe" (p. 133). He illustrates this point with a childhood anecdote:

> When I was about fourteen years of age [I had an experience that] deeply influenced my whole life. A necessity I could not understand swept over me: I had to try again and again to imagine the edge of space, or its edgelessness, time with a beginning and an end or a time without beginning or end, and both were equally impossible, equally hopeless—yet there seemed to be only the choice between the one or the other absurdity. Under an irresistible compulsion I reeled from one to the other, at times so closely threatened with the danger of madness that I seriously thought of avoiding it by suicide. (p. 136)

That Buber's struggle is not unique among those who have achieved distinction is well documented. Einstein, for example, was said to have formulated his discoveries in near hallucinatory flights of fancy (Arieti 1976). Dali, Van Gogh, and Holderlin appear to have been inspired by psychotic-like visions (Arieti 1976, Prentky 1979). Blake, who wrote that "the road to excess leads to the palace of wisdom," may well have been afflicted with schizophrenia (May 1969). Numerous other historical titans have tangled with similar constrictive or expansive surpluses. Manic-depressive qualities appear to have been integral to the works of poets Robert Lowell and Sylvia Plath, psychologist William James, and philosopher Arthur Schopenhauer (Leo 1984, May 1969). Schizoid, histrionic, and epileptic dispositions seem to have influenced the creations of Nietzsche, Beethoven, Michelangelo, Byron, and Heine (Prentky 1979). Obsessive-compulsive meticulousness, or what Prentky terms "a seeming encyclopedic grasp of all historical and current thought in a given area" (1979, p. 18), appear to characterize the labors of Robert Oppenheimer, Tycho Brahe, and E.O. Lawrence.

The aspiration toward greatness, then, gives rise to a dilemma: the further one ventures forth, the more one risks destabilization; the closer one approaches endlessness, the more one faces destruction. There is a magnificent scene in the movie *The Shining* (based on the Stephen King novel) that very well illuminates this problem. *The Shining* opens with a long, breathtaking swoop of a lonely country road. The road wends its way through several cavernous valleys. It is wintertime, still and crisp. As the camera pans the vast spiraling vista, I am left with many reflections about splendor. The mountainous grandeur of the scene is daunting. It makes me anticipate that many monumental struggles lie ahead, many upheavals. The long winding road, the illimitable terrain, each bespeak a sense of directionlessness and of untamed forces. The stillness, shadows, and cavernous depths, on the other hand, convey a sense of unease, of impenetrable secrecy and mischief. In some ways they are more unsettling than their majestic counterparts, as they mute the puzzlements that they imply. I feel bottomless in their midst.

Like life, this scene makes me an offer. It invites me to explore the chasms and meandering paths. It stimulates my sense of adventure, curiosity, and desire; and it places me at a crossroads.

Now it is apparent that we are all at this crossroads. We have the choice to *renounce* such invitations (in the form of despair) or *indulge* in them (in the form of fanaticism). But these alternatives are basically defensive: renunciation guards against the unbearability of indulgence, and indulgence protects against the banality of renunciation. The best way to work out of this dilemma, classic horror indicates, is to reject both polarities and adopt the third alternative of wonderment. Returning to the aforementioned movie scene, wonderment would imply that I climb at least *some* of the jagged terrain, walk *part of the way* along the road, and savor *segments* of the unfolding mystery. The risks, of course, would echo those of our previously mentioned lovers, creators, and geniuses. They would be formidable, but they would not reach the heights of those posed by classic horror. They would resonate more with Van Helsing, in other words, than with Scottie, Frankenstein, or Jekyll.

Wonderment dictates that I risk the fall, the dizziness, and even the collapse from exhaustion. It dictates that I *engage* the spectacle before me but not without essential resources—wit, preparation, and cognizance of my limits. The wonderer must be "hard," as Nietzsche declared, but must also eschew rashness. Such a person must be persistently leery of pat solutions, or exaggerated anticipations, and acknowledge the paradoxes, complexities, and surprises of life. "The strength of a spirit," Nietzsche (1886/1966) elucidates, "might be measured according to how much of the 'truth' he would be able to stand—more clearly, to what degree it would *need* to be watered down, shrouded, sweetened, blunted, and falsified" (p. 49).

The "truth" for the wonderer is that presented in the classic tales we have reviewed. The value of these tales is that they prompt us to reflect. Shelley, Stoker, Stevenson, et al. are not, I believe, trying to make us cynical about the world; they are also not attempting to encourage anarchy. They are attempting something much more ambitious: to boldly outline the human condition (so far as has been grasped) and to summarize the alternatives therein. This quest has led them to a plea for wonderment, a plea that we learn how to *participate* in subtle, sensual, and intricate practices, without inevitably *fixating* on such practices; or *share* in global ambitions without necessarily *indulging* in them. A highly observant former mental patient, Norma MacDonald (1979), spoke about this spirit in connection with schizophrenia, but she might as well have been discussing human potentiality in general: "Living with [my] illness," she writes, "is a matter of balancing opposites which are enormously incompatible" (p. 112). And yet "I began to see that

> . . . I had much more than a handicap—I had a tool and potential. This sort of mind, controlled and used, has a far-reaching imaginative power, a deep instinctual awareness, and the ability to understand a wide span of emotional and intellectual experiences. Perhaps in ten or twenty more years I will be able to control it much better than I do now (p. 113)

Perhaps each of us, thanks to the recognition of wonderment, will be able to nurture the marvelous in the maddening and the maddening in the marvelous, to achieve fuller lives. Perhaps we will strive, like Norma MacDonald—who echoes Nietzsche—to become passionate people who master our passions (See Kaufmann 1968, p. 280).

Wonderment in Science

*Strange that science, which in the old
days seemed harmless, should have
evolved into a nightmare that causes
everyone to tremble.*

—ALBERT EINSTEIN

It has been a long time, it seems to me, since Western science has celebrated wonderment. That mix of awe and doubt, marvel and skepticism, so integral to such luminaries as Einstein, have gone the way of the horse and buggy. Today, there is but one undeniable trend—technocratization. There are, of course, mobilizations against this trend, but they have yet to significantly cohere. The management of society by technicians, to the contrary, is *institutionalized* (Rifkin 1983).

To be sure, technocracy has its place. It has helped combat disease, increase mobility, and expand industrial and agricultural production. It has helped us to live more *comfortably*. But there are two basic dangers connected to this "comfort," and classic horror has alerted us to each; the first concerns presumption (or what the Greeks termed, "hubris"), the second concerns banality.

The first danger I refer to, scientific hubris, can be readily grasped. It can be seen in the rush to exploit fossil fuels, the indifference toward air and water supplies, and the dependence upon nuclear output. The Bhopal chemical spill, Chernobyl, the Exxon Valdez, beachside medical waste, radioactive dumping, the greenhouse effect, and depletion of the ozone layer are but a few of the unforeseen consequences of these policies. The obvious question, accordingly, is what in the world brought us to this point? Or to put it in the language of classic horror, what made us "meddle in things men should leave alone"?

While the answer to this question is far from definitive, the lessons of classic horror—especially as they apply to science—can be illuminating. Fanatical overreaching, they imply, is a product of some form of panic. Frankenstein panicked over his (and his culture's) sense of imperfection; Dracula panicked over the decimation of his ancient kinsmen; the Invisible Man became alarmed by his vocational inferiority; Mr. Hyde recoiled at his suffocating Victorianism; Dr. Morbius reacted against his human frailty; the robotic saboteur in *Alien,* finally, panicked in the service of his greedy programers.

What then drives real scientists to despotic lengths? Clearly, they are some of the same incitements that prod the a-bove "monstrosities"—inadequacies, self-devaluations, financial want, vengefulnesses of all kinds. But thus far we have only been speaking about the dramatic cases, the *individuals* who end up in court battles or who star on the evening news. We can point to these people and accuse them of being our Frankensteins or Hydes. Yet what of the vast majority of scientists and technocrats who do not achieve, but nevertheless associate with, this notoriety or infamy? What are we to make of them? What of the specialists who approve of the ill-fated products, or the vendors who sell the products, or the laborers who assist in their manufacture? What of the *organizations* which support and legitimize the products? Are they not also Frankensteinian and accountable to similar standards?

The question of *organizational* monstrosity is one of the most pressing of our time—this is so not only because of its insidiousness, its resistance to detection, but also its lethality. Only in the rarest circumstance can an individual wreak the havoc that a given industry can perpetrate. An entire network of industries or a professional field, on the other hand, can generate immeasurable harm.

In order to grasp the dimensions of this problem, it is useful to turn again to the nonfiction paragon of horror—Nazism. One of the most harrowing revelations to emerge from this era—much to the dismay of intellectuals—is that *professionals,* not rank-and-file party members, were the prime Nazi "innovators" (Hilberg, quoted in Moyers 1988, p. 10). Indeed, the final solution to rid the state of Jews was systematically engineered by lawyers, military bosses, and physicians. What went awry? What prompted the most educated minds in Germany to sterilize, kill, and disable, to butcher "experimental" subjects, and to produce gases, ovens, and other instruments of mass destruction?

The Nazi Doctors (1986), a seminal work by Robert Lifton, comes about as close as any study has, I believe, to answering this puzzle, and partially draws its insights from classic horror (see p. 429). Lifton, for example, shows how respected citizens, such as physicians, become merciless killers in large part because of what their culture becomes, because of what Lifton refers to as a "double" identity. They become Frankensteins and Hydes, in other words, because it is culturally sanctioned to do so. It is culturally sanctioned to defend against perceived weaknesses (in the case of Germany, the post-World War I Depression). These citizens can therefore maintain *both* their professional identity *and* barbarous nationalistic identity, without being aware of any discrepancy. For some Germans this meant that being a "good" doctor and ridding the world of Jewish "pollution" were synonymous, or that being a physician to the "volk" squared with eliminating the non-Aryan "cancer" from the "German national body" (see Lifton 1986, pp. 30 and 477).

Such forms of "doubling," as Lifton (1986, p. 429) calls them, are echoed by the "noble" scientific intentions of Frankenstein, Jekyll, and Morbius, the "justified" vengefulness of the Phantom and the Invisible Man, and the "sincere" romanticism of *Vertigo's* Scottie.

It is in light of these stories, accordingly, that we can better understand the subtleties of scientific hubris. We can better understand the impotence and rationalization that underlie it. This impotence manifests itself as a kind of individual and collective jealousy, a jealousy of infinitude, if you will. As a result, too many scientists become aggressive toward infinitude, try to domesticate and take it over. They try to control it as if it were an object in their laboratory, as if it had clearly definable parameters and predictable effects. The consequence of their actions, of course, is anything but predictable.

A degree of technology is essential in modern society, and some price must inevitably be paid for it. But the counsels of classic horror are clear: be wary of desperate or panic-driven visions—too often they are as gratuitous as they are grotesque.

While some scientists are envious of and strive to *subsume* infinitude, others shy away from it and strive to blunt its impact. This is the problem, to which we now turn, of scientific banality.

I am concerned, for example, about the tradition of atomizing and minimizing in my own field of psychology. "When man was tragic," as Rollo May (1967) put it,

> [we] made him trivial. When he suffered passively, [we] described him as simpering; and when he drummed up enough courage to act, [we] called it stimulus and response. (p. 4)

That this tradition shows no sign of abating is attested to by a recent article in the premier journal of the American Psychological Association. Here, three researchers were given "Distinguished Scientific Awards for an Early Career Contribution to Psychology." The following is a rough sample of their subjects: (1) "Toward an information processing analysis of depression"; (2) "Depression and information processing: Self-schemata and the encoding of self-relevant information"; (3) "Intracortical connections and their physiological correlates in the primary auditory cortex (AI) in the cat"; (4) "Extending the limits of complex learning in organic amnesia: Computer training in a vocational domain" (*American Psychologist* 1991, pp. 302, 303, and 305).

Now I do not condemn the contents of these contributions; they are undoubtedly useful within their spheres of application. However, I do take exception to the *way* in which these contents are treated. The message is that (1) American psychology places a premium upon physicalistic and measurable properties of human functioning, and (2) this is the ideological standard by which young and future-oriented scholars are to be gauged.

But "twice-two-makes-four is not life, gentlemen," as Dostoyevsky once put it—not life, let alone psychology. "It is the beginning of death" (quoted in Friedman 1964, p. 62). It is the beginning of a deep cynicism about the human reach. This cynicism, moreover, can be seen every time missiles are discussed as if they were bargaining chips or when civilian war casualties are described as "collateral damage." It can be seen in the objectification of the body, the quantification of nature, and the intellectualization of spirit. It can be tasted, finally, in our horror stories, which vehemently caution us against such debasement.

Recall, for example, Midge's comparison of a bra to a cantilever bridge in *Vertigo,* or Lanyon's equation of love with "sobriety" in *Jekyll and Hyde,* or the ornithologist's "knowledge" in *The Birds.* Each is a retreat from the horrific complexity of our condition, but equally, sadly, the holy radiance as well.

Thanks to technocracy, on the other hand, such debasement is not likely to lessen. Hiding is simply too easy—behind masses of regulation, volumes of jargon, and miles of concrete. Burrowing into specialties or "programs" is the opiate of the culture. The automation of life, in other words—packaging, appearance, and instant results—is the raging new standard.

Two scientific tendencies, accordingly, punctuate modern life—exasperation and grandiosity. Exasperation shirks from, and grandiosity presumes, infinitude. Each, moreover, is a reaction to the other. Exasperation fuels grandiosity, and grandiosity collapses back into exasperation. Speeding the operation of this cycle is a vast armamentarium of mental and physical *mechanisms.* Such mechanisms delude the grandiose into believing that they can transcend, and the exasperated into believing that they can embed. But is it not more fulfilling to be more like the Persian in *Phantom of the Opera,* for example, than Erik or the managers? Is it not more useful, in the long run, to *survey* rather than dissect, to *appreciate* rather than objectify, and to *propose* rather than insist? Is it not the means (as much as the ends) and the ethics (as much as the results) that redeem in scientific research?

Hence, it is precisely this humanistic-scientific blend that wonderment celebrates. It is precisely this consensus-based, participatory science that is upheld by classic horror. While scientific wonderment is "messier" than its counterparts, it is more respectful of life. It is much closer to, although methodologically different from, art. It aims not for prediction and control but for understanding and socially conscious application.

Wonderment in Religion

The religious geniuses of history have argued that to be really submissive means to be submissive to the highest power, the true infinity, the absolute— and not to any human substitutes, lovers, leaders, nation-states.

—ERNEST BECKER

At what point does one relinquish one's power? This is the central problem of religion, which quite literally means *religare* —to "bind back" (Webster's 1968, p. 1228). Put another way, religion is the shape or design of one's life. It is the container of one's dearest projects. The question is, how liberating is this container? How faithful is it to one personally and to humankind as a whole? Classic horror steeps us in such queries.

The first question that classic horror confronts, fittingly, is what makes a given religion virtuous? What, in other words, makes it a dignifying, optimizing affair—respectful of the human situation? The answer, once again, is founded upon wonderment. For example, it is wonderment that intensifies the ordinary, awakens the senses, and sparks the imagination. It is wonderment that moves people to serve their fellows, celebrate nature, and learn from and embrace diversity. In short, it is wonderment that beckons us to infinitize, as Kierkegaard might have said. On the other hand, wonderment alerts us to the perils of such forays as well. It posts signs and warnings to help us *navigate* our journey. These signs and warnings, in classic horror, take the form of monstrosities. Colossal beings, proliferating life-forms, and cosmic calamities, for example, alert us to hyperexpansive life-designs; while secret forces, creeping maladies, and transparent entities caution us about hyperconstrictive life-designs. At the same time, it is important to remember just how rarely such extremities actually manifest in the horror narrative. For as much as our tales initiate us in the perversities, they also bathe us in the majesties, and this part must be equally recognized. I would even go so far as to say that *most* of our experiences with classic horror are composed of thrills—hunting, searching, or creating; only at the fringes do such thrills turn monstrous. The lesson of classic horror, then, is a challenging one. It invites us to both test and heed our psychophysical limits. It provides few blueprints for the engagement of these limits; their shape is left to us. All that is asked is that we genuinely *grapple* with the circumstances arrayed before us and neither deny nor flaunt them.

The seeds of this conception, ironically enough, derive from traditionally religious, not merely artistic, sources (see Smith 1986). Yet we are justified in asking, what happened to them? What happened, for example, to Job's titanic struggle with a thoroughly enigmatic God, or Vishnu's injunction against divine knowledge (Otto 1958, p. 188)? What happened to Rabbi Hillel's and Jesus' admonishments to love the stranger, or to Buddha's uncertainty about the eternal? What happened to Muhammad's religious tolerance?

What happens to most radical and demanding ideas? They become marginalized. They become marginalized, moreover, by a fretful world, a world starving for structure, guidance, and *salvation*. How many contemporary religions, for example, *encourage*—not merely permit—interreligious exchange, or passionately critique (as well as affirm) their own teachings, or relegate decision-making to their adherents?

The answer, of course, is few; and yet it is precisely such "oddities" in religious life that the originators proposed. It is precisely wonderment upon which the "high" religions have been forged. Origins aside, though, the high religions did not and probably could not embrace wonderment. There are several major reasons for this. First, the majority of those attracted to the high religions were oppressed. Oppressed people generally seek comfort, not challenge and suspense; and the greater the oppression, moreover, the greater the tendency to require sectarian ideologies. The sentiment *"We* are the chosen ones" or *"Our* God is supreme" has an undeniable appeal to downtrodden ears. Another reason that wonderment could not endure is because of the eventual institution of authoritarian command structures. Like the adherents noted above, many of those associated with such structures would use religion to shield as well as lionize their statures. If power corrupts and absolute power corrupts absolutely, then what position could be more corruptible than such power in domains that profess to speak to so many aspects of an adherent's life? A religion of wonderment, on the other hand, would wholeheartedly resist such clerical ambitiousness. Above and beyond these reasons, however, wonderment itself was resisted because of an implication so radical that it may not have even been clear to those who conceived it. This is the paradox that religious prophecy implies a nonreligious (nonsectarian and nonabsolutist) integrationism, which emphasizes compassion and a respect for mystery.[5] That these features parallel the tone and moral insight of classic horror is not entirely lost upon those disciples who have toiled to suppress such notions. For them this paradox *is a horror,* outright and unabashed. Nevertheless, there it stands—a plausible extrapolation of prophecy.

While a few contemporary religious thinkers, such as Paul Tillich and Martin Buber, genuinely grapple with wonderment,[6] many do not. For example, many in the so-called New Age and mystical communities question the traditionalists but then perpetuate their resistance to wonderment (see Zweig and Abrams 1991). In particular, they profess eclecticism—pantheism, paganism, an assortment of Eastern doctrines—but often end up factionalized. The effect, as in traditional religiosity, is both to prematurely cut off and extol human potentiality. In the case of some New Age movements, for example, potentiality is curbed by the object of worship—crystals, spirit guides, gurus, deities, and so forth. Ostensibly loving and accepting, these objects or beings may not, in fact, tolerate dissenting perspectives. They are loving and accepting as long as one *agrees* or *complies* with them; but if one questions them, one courts trouble in the form of ostracism or "excommunication." This trouble takes two other forms as well: disillusionment and victimization (for example, see Butler 1991 on the recent tragedies in the American Buddhist community and Babbs 1991 on "New Age Fundamentalism"). At the same time, many find New Age sectarianism to be psychospiritually aggrandizing; adherents can feel righteous and self-assured in their matrilineal, patrilineal, material, or spiritual niche.

With regard to certain mystical positions, on the other hand, there is a more subtle abnegation of wonderment. This abnegation culminates in a form of surrender. The question is, when does one cosmically surrender, and what does such an act imply? If surrender means renunciation of one's powers to question, then is it perhaps *unduly* restrictive? How useful, for example, is it for a mystic to affirm "suchness" (the idea that all is the way it cosmically should be) in a time of war or oppression? Should tyrannical leaderships be "accepted"? Should abusive relationships be "tolerated"? Should reckless and irresponsible politicians—who accomplish nothing for the public welfare—be disregarded? How much "trust" should the mystic place in existence, to "work things out"? The tragic case of Osel Tendzin, leader of one of the largest Buddhist communities in America, is representative of the difficulties posed by some forms of mystical surrender. In December 1988, Tendzin admitted that he had been infected with the AIDS virus for three years, that he continued to have intercourse during that period, and that he neglected to inform and protect his partners (Butler 1991). His justification? "Thinking I had some extraordinary means of protection," Tendzin was reported to have stated, "I went ahead with my business as if something would take care of it for me" (Butler 1991, p. 138). Tendzin's predecesor, Chogyam Trungpa, was no less compromised by his own destructive behavior: "Trungpa Rinpoche said that because he had *Vajra nature* [a yogically transformed and stabilized psychophysiology], he was immune to the normal physiological effects of alcohol" (Butler 1991, p. 141). Yet neither Trungpa nor Tendzin were immune; they too readily "gave up."

On the other hand, they too readily flattered themselves as well. The logic seems to go something like this: if I merge with all there is, then I must (in a psychological sense, at least) *become* all there is. If I become all there is, then my power is unstinting. Yet not only does this attitude encourage undue *self*-aggrandizement, it encourages undue beliefs about cosmic consciousness.[7] The question is, how much can one infer truth, understanding, or power from the unitive experience? To what extent does it prompt self-assured claims about health, leadership, and morality, or accessibility to knowledge, purity, and privilege? In short, to what degree does the unitive experience lead to psychosocial *polarization,* as opposed to reflection, dialogue, and interplay (see Schneider 1987, 1989)?

"Now from my own unforgettable experience," elaborates Buber (1965),

> I know well that there is a state in which the bonds of the personal nature of life seem to have fallen away from us and we experience undivided unity. But I do not know—what the soul willingly imagines and indeed is bound to imagine (mine too once did!)—that in this I had attained to a union with the primal being or the godhead. That is an exaggeration no longer permitted to the responsible understanding. (p. 24)

The dream sequence in *Vertigo* touched upon earlier also cautions against "exaggeration." Scottie (the dreamer) perceives a vivid bouquet of flowers. This bouquet parallels the one that Madeline held when he first met her, when all seemed attainable. It also evokes a certain mystical sensation. As the petals peel away Scottie finds himself beginning to unravel. Next, he stands next to Carlotta, Madeline's beatific incarnation. Then, he finds himself falling, just as Madeline/Carlotta had fallen earlier in the story. Finally, he approaches Madeline/Carlotta's gravesite. He is about to leap into it when we have a realization: Scottie's flowery, beatific romance has become unsteadying and bizarre. Suddenly, Scottie plunges into the cosmic pit and attempts, in effect, to consummate his adoration. Yet Hitchcock (with other practioners in the classic horror genre) is doubtful of the possibilities of such a consummation. He implies, in fact, that it is a deception, that completion is a deception. This is borne out in the final sequence where, despite Scottie's efforts to merge, he *spirals,* endlessly into space!

One might object at this point that the only reason Scottie becomes destablized by this experience is because he is ill-prepared to handle the metaphysical. Properly trained mystics, on the other hand, would be able to "relax into" and embrace Scottie's cosmological journey. Perhaps; but classic horror always wants to inquire, "to what extent?" Dr. Morbius and the Krell could also probably assimilate more of the cosmic than Scottie, but not indefinitely. There is a vast difference, classic horror reminds us (as Buber does), between a *sense* of the boundless and the unconditional absorption of Being. Tales like *Vertigo* help us to perceive this distinction.

The spiritual challenge of classic horror, then, is wonderment. Wonderment affirms the radical "foundations" of the great religions but warns against two subsequent developments —the tendencies either to preempt or to exaggerate human potentiality. Too many of us are susceptible to these tendencies, and too many religions are ready to accommodate our susceptibility. Because people forget paradox, however, preemption and exaggeration will only lead to dysfunction. This is illustrated by the traditional preoccupation with codes, for example, which ignore our ability to self-direct, or the insistence upon righteousness, on the other hand, which overlooks our fallibility.

At the same time, though, to what degree do *anti*religious movements neutralize such polarizations? Is the atheistic response productive?

The consensus of classic horror, as with other "tragic" purviews, is that atheism courts the same problems. We have already considered the reductionist effects of science and technology, which parallel the reductionisms of certain religious traditions, but there are numerous other atheistic devaluations that can be cited. The banning of cultural and religious practices (as in some authoritarian or totalitarian states), the "leveling" effects of mass-market consumerism (as in many industrialized nations), and the relativizing of ideas (as in deconstructionist philosophy, for example) are among them.

Fanatical sectarianism, on the other hand, is also not unknown to atheists. For example, how many among them worship the dollar bill or the latest gadget? How many bow to advertising, sports heroes, or industrialists? How many adore the state, the race, or the political ideology? How many are addicted to drugs, organizations, or jobs? "Something is holy to everyone," Tillich (1967) keenly observes, "even to those who deny the holy" (p. 130).

To conclude, so many of us, both secular and religious, continue to seek guarantees: God, the state, the machine, the lover, the job—*it* will ultimately come through, *it* will shield us from chaos, *it* will charge us with glory. But at what cost, we must always inquire? Wonderment reminds us that, yes, we all need something to save or justify our lives; the question is, who or what? What do we affirm, and what do we give up?

Although the monster tale does not specifically answer these queries, it does suggest an approach to the questions. It suggests that human being, in its starkness, is *both* freeing *and* limiting. Compromise either of these dimensions, and one compromises vitality. It is no surprise that monstrosity is fascinating: Frankenstein is a savant, Dracula is elegant, the Phantom is masterful. They and others like them alert us to the miraculous in life—the dimensions of dazzlement, complexity, and adventure. It is of equal significance, on the other hand, that such figures become grotesque at certain points. They *overreach* in some fashion. The lesson, therefore, is to steer between these modalities, to *respect* them.

"Respect" is the key term here, for it is precisely what banal and fanatical religions lack. Either we are perfect or we are pitiful, these teachings imply; combinations of the perfect and the pitiful are scorned. Yet the universe, as classic horror contends, is a very muddled phenomenon. It may or may not ultimately favor us; it may not even ultimately sanction life. The best we can do, therefore, is to respect these conditions—the tremendous energies of Creation—while at the same time acknowledging our own. This implies a pragmatic vision, but it does not have to be a "cold" or excessively intellectualized vision. To the contrary, classic horror promotes a "round," rich pragmatism, which draws not merely from intellectual but from emotional and intuitive sources as well. While such a framework cannot *definitively* differentiate moral from immoral acts or useful from nonuseful experiences, it does not leave us bereft, either. To the contrary, it recommends to us that *emotional and intuitive resonance, coupled with intellectual analysis,* are the best evaluative criteria that we presently possess. Others may argue the case differently, but they will be hard-pressed to match the intensity, relevancy, and scope of these criteria.[8]

Horror's vision, accordingly, is based on respect. It respects the electrifying but also the humbling, the resonant but also the analytical, and the diverse but simultaneously the cohesive. It is up to *us,* the vision implies, to decide our place in this menagerie; *we* must work out the design.

Circle Limit IV (1960), M. C. Escher. © 1960 M. C. Escher/Cordon Art, Baarn, Holland.

Epilogue: A Comment on Evil

The poetry of transgression is also knowledge. He who transgresses not only breaks a rule. He goes somewhere that others are not; and he knows something the others don't know.

—SUSAN SONTAG

[The] gain of infinity is never attained except through despair.

—SØREN KIERKEGAARD

We are now in a position to put our findings together. What does horror imply about the most pressing concern of our time—human and nonhuman *evil?*

Before we discuss this complex topic, some background may be helpful. Let us consider how other thoughtful writers have defined evil. Contemporary essayist Lance Morrow (1991), for example, perceives evil as "a monster." "It has a strange coercive force," he elaborates, "a temptation, a mystery, a horrible charm" (p. 49); elsewhere, following Milton, he suggests that the devil can be more interesting than God. Rollo May (1969) understands evil as the "daemonic"—a destructive or constructive "power." Buddha appears to have equated evil with greed and desire; Augustine, on the other hand, compared it to privation and nothingness. Some Old Testament writers, finally, conceived of Satan as evil incarnate, others as God's and humanity's "adversary" (Reese 1980).

The lesson of classic horror, I believe, is that evil pertains to all of these dimensions—monstrosity, charm, power, desire, privation, opposition—but transcends them as well. For evil, according to classic horror, is constrictive or expansive *excess;* it is infinitude which cannot be managed. Consider, for example, the assortment of external events that uphold this conception— earthquakes, floods, volcanos, disease, all those circumstances that associate with the uncheckable. Mind you, I am not saying that such circumstances are inherently evil or cruel; how can we know this? What I am proposing, however, is that they *become* evil at the point where we can no longer assimilate them, at the point where they feel *bottomless.* Evil, as conceived by classic horror, then, is the inability to *handle* constrictive or expansive endlessness; it is not the endlessness itself.

This contention holds true for the realm of human evil as well. Who, for example, can "handle" the gulag, Auschwitz, or a bout of schizophrenia? Who can countenance the constrictive and expansive outrages of our fictional monsters? At the same time, is it not these very same terrors that give rise to our villians and monsters in the first place? Reflect, for example, on the chaos-phobic technocrat or the impotence-riddled fanatic; consider the woe-driven lives of Dracula, the Phantom, the Invisible Man, and Frankenstein's monster.

As long as there is fear, therefore, there will be evil; as long as there are portions of ourselves and the world that we cannot absorb, there will be maneuvers aimed at distancing and protecting ourselves from those realities—even if these maneuvers are as destructive as the realities which they fend off. But if evil, as we have defined it, is inescapable, it is also curiously inviting. It is the horizon—albeit misapplied in many cases—of our furthermost possibilities. The question is, to what extent can we beneficially engage these possibilities, to what extent can we *cultivate* them?

While we have yet to realize the fruits that these challenges hold out, there are, I believe, reasons for hope. This century, for example, has witnessed the most abominable fulfillments of horror's prophecies to date: massive secular and religious hate movements, unchecked developments in nuclear and non-nuclear weaponry, runaway environmental abuses, and ballooning generations of gluttons and addicts. At the same time, however, this century has witnessed Gandhi and Martin Luther

King Jr., the toppling of monarchies, the crippling of tyrannical industrialists, and most recently, the dismemberment of Marxist-Leninist totalitarianism.

We are now on the threshold of a postmodern age, an age of deconstructed truths and dismantled authorities. While we are freed by this development to a certain extent, we are also simultaneously threatened by it. We are threatened by the very lapses into extravagance that postmodernism has prided itself on thwarting. The problem, of course, is that postmodernism may forget its *own* inclinations to excess, its own driven and defensive qualities. Among these are an aversion to classicism (in myriad, cross-disciplinary forms), an inclination toward anarchy, and a dilution of the personal sense of self.

These are the circumstances, accordingly, that we are now called upon to confront. Can wonderment prevail? Can paradox triumph? Possibly. But if they do, it will not be because of sugar-coated platitudes or "can do" formulas. It will be because of hard and deep searches into our beings, numerous clashes with our ideals, and daring encounters with others. It will, in large measure, be attributable to that great undervalued body of wisdom with which we have dealt—classic horror and tragic art.

Notes

Preface

1. See the discussion of "cosmic fear" in Lovecraft's *Supernatural Horror in Literature* (New York: Dover, 1973). See also Phillip Hallie's *The Paradox of Cruelty* (Middletown, CT: Wesleyan University Press, 1969), pp. 63–84, and David Hartwell's Introduction to *Foundations of Fear* (New York: Tom Doherty Associates, 1992).

2. See my book *The Paradoxical Self: Toward an Understanding of Our Contradictory Nature* (New York: Plenum/Insight, 1990).

3. From Holderlin's poem entitled "Patmos."

Introduction—Ecstasy, Terror, and Infinity

1. The original meaning of the term "holy," according to leading theologian Rudolf Otto (1923/1958, p. 12), is *mysterium tremendum* (or "tremendous mystery") and only later acquired moral and aesthetic significance. Note also the dual connotation of "holy"—as in "hole" and "whole."

2. I distinguish "terror" from "horror" in this book in the following way: "terror" emphasizes the fear of *literal* infinitude (for example, massive or imperceptible objects), "horror" emphasizes *symbolic* or figurative intimations of infinitude (the dark castle in *Dracula* or the winding staircase in *Vertigo*). In the former case, the emphasis is on the *object* of one's fear; in the latter it is on the *connotations* of the object of one's fear. While horror stories generally employ combinations of the above two elements, the better ones, in my opinion, accentuate the symbolic. Because it utilizes one's imagination, symbolic horror enriches and vivifies the experience of the observer; literal terror,

on the other hand, as a spate of contemporary movies attest, is usually visceral and fleeting.

3. John Donne (quoted in R.D. Stock, *The holy and the daemonic from Sir Thomas Brown to William Blake*, Princeton, NJ: Princeton University Press, 1982, p. 22). See also Milan Kundera's *The Art of the Novel* (New York: Harper & Row, 1986).

4. I refer here to that cluster of literature which can broadly be called "existential." See for example Kundera's *The Art of the Novel;* Ernest Becker's *Denial of Death* (New York: Free Press, 1973); Walter Kaufmann's *From Shakespeare to Existentialism* (New York: Anchor Books, 1960); William James's *Pragmatism and Other Essays* (New York: Washington Square Press, 1963); Rollo May's *The Cry for Myth* (New York: Norton, 1991); and my own *The Paradoxical Self: Toward an Understanding of our Contradictory Nature* (New York: Plenum, 1990) for support for this point.

While I fully acknowledge the unprovability of my assumptions, significant light, I believe, can be shed on their *utility*. For what is at stake here, it may be clear, is nothing less than the competing philosophies of inquiry and certainty and their wealth of psychosocial implications. I will address these implications in the last chapter.

I The Structure of Horror: Chaos and Obliteration

1. See Otto Rank's brilliant notion of a "psychology of difference" in *Beyond Psychology* (New York: Dover, 1958).

2. This distinction may explain the relief we feel when a mystery, real-life or fictional, is solved. It also may explain the eventual tedium we feel when we witness graphic horror.

3. In his psychoanalytically-based *Dreadful Pleasures* (New York: Oxford University Press, 1985), Paul Twitchell also suggests that classic horror highlights juvenile (rather than "mature") themes. Such tales, he believes, are aimed at pubescent audiences because they address an issue—the incest taboo—which pertains directly to those audiences. Yet this thesis, I believe, does not do justice to the wealth of *adult* interest in classic horror, nor does it address the myths, tragedies, and

suspense stories that both inspired and succeeded the so-called adolescent tales—consider, for example, the works of Homer, Shakespeare, and Hitchcock. Contrasting his thesis to those who perceive an element of the cosmic in classic horror, Twitchell (1985, p. 11) writes, "my concerns are thankfully less transcendental"—but they are also less convincing, I believe, because of this very omission.

4. Jung does not always seem to be consistent on this point, but even when he stresses cosmic dread, there is a hint of idealization in his commentary. On the one hand, for example, he implies that the Self is as chaotic and forbidding as the Gnostic God Abraxas; on the other, he suggests that one can (ultimately) unify and "reconcile" this Self (see Jung 1961 on "wholeness," and Hoeller 1982 on the "Pleroma" of Abraxas).

II Wisdom-Horror:
Dracula and *Frankenstein*

1. The Bible, and Oriental scriptures as well, are rife with chaotic and obliterating deities (see Otto 1958). Consider, for example, the roles of such deities in Noah and the ark, Job, Jonah and the big fish, the plagues in Egypt, and Armageddon; stories as well about the Void, Vishnu, Kali, and Allah. Even the so-called neolithic era (which antedates 3000 B.C.E.) is punctuated by such awe-filling scenarios. The womb, for example, is believed to have symbolized the "Great Goddess," creator and destroyer of life, in neolithic cultures (Gimbutas 1989, p. 316).

Beyond these initial similarities, however, such parables and classic horror differ in one major respect: *the faith or ultimate trust one can place in Existence.* Whereas religious epics almost invariably affirm this trust (as in the lament "God works in mysterious ways"), classic horror rarely displays such confidence. We will explore the implications of this issue in the final chapter.

H.P. Lovecraft, it should be further noted, is one of the few essayists to have fully grasped the transcendental significance of classic horror. "The one test of the really weird," he writes in *Supernatural Horror in Literature* (1973), is . . . whether or not there be excited in the reader a profound sense of dread, and of contact with unknown spheres and powers; a subtle attitude of awed listening, as if for the beating of black wings or the scratching of outside shapes and entities on the known universe's utmost rim. And of course, the more completely and unifiedly a story conveys this atmosphere, the better it is as a work of art. (p. 16)

IV Horror as a Worldview

1.   See my reflections on the Persian Gulf war, *New Age or "New Order"?*, in the Association for Humanistic Psychology newsletter, *Perspectives,* March/April 1991 or a summarized version which appeared in the American Psychological Association *Monitor,* April 1991.

2.   Let me be clear that by wonderment I am not speaking about some kind of sedate normalcy, which writers such as Stephen King (1983), Walter Kendrick (1991), and Phillip Hallie (1969) seem to uphold as the moral object of classic horror—I am speaking about a dynamic, *paradoxical* engagement of life. See my *Paradoxical Self* (1990) for a further elucidation of this concept.

Although classic horror has cautionary elements and ostensibly "happy" endings, it is simplistic to characterize the genre as an apologia for conservative values. Monsters, for example, sometimes perish in classic horror, but their associations with instability and groundlessness endure. The moral tone of classic horror, likewise, is sometimes traditional, but it is also distinctively revolutionary, as we have seen.

3.   I frankly cannot understand Carroll's (1990, p. 240) objection (which he ties to Kant) to the sublimeness implied by ostensibly maddening or repulsive states. His (and Kant's) view strikes me as overly sanitized, and it also neglects abundant sources of empirical data. For example, he does not explain the mass *excitement* over violent sports, battles, or contests; he overlooks our *fascination* with mental and physical aberration—decay, deformation, anguish, and eccentricity. In short, I believe these theorists miss the vital connection, so well depicted by such

luminaries as Nietzsche (1872/1956), Artaud (1976) and Bataille (1973), between disgust, excess, and infinitude.

4. If ever there was a doubt about the power of excess or monstrosity to compel, Hitler's Germany and Stalin's Russia have firmly dispelled it. Consider, for example, their massive buildings of state, block-long banners, and garish displays of military might; consider also their bone-chilling monuments to Aryan and Communist patronage and their solemn flirtations with the occult. How many have prostrated themselves before these extravagances? How many have readied their weapons?

5. Some would call this perspective "spiritual" as opposed to "religious" (because of its relative lack of structure). However, "spirituality" in certain quarters has become associated with almost as much factionalization as religion in recent years. Witness, for example, the implicit sectarianism in some of the "New Age" spiritual movements, as we shall discuss. For this reason and those previously noted, I prefer the term "wonderment"—rather than "spirituality"—to describe non-formal transcendental states.

6. I refer here to Tillich's (1952) concept of "the faith to doubt" and Buber's (1964) notion of "holy insecurity." See also Ram Dass's recent (1992) foray into wonderment, *Compassion in Action: Setting Out on the Path of Service* (New York: Crown).

7. This is not to suggest that "giving up" (cosmically) is unimportant. Clearly, it can profoundly reconstitute our lives. The concern of classic horror, however, is with our *conception* of "giving up." Do we view it as a crutch—or as a final, humbling act? a cure—or a bridge to something more?

8. A colleague of mine, Tad Goguen-Frantz, suggested that moral and ethical acts be judged, at least partially, on the basis of what she termed "resonance" validity, which is very similar to the criteria I set forth here. William James's (1963) notion of "radical empiricism" is also highly pertinent.

Bibliography

Arieti, S. (1976). *Creativity: The magic synthesis.* New York: Basic Books.

Artaud, A. (1976). *Antonin Artaud: selected writings.* New York: Farrar, Strauss, & Giroux.

Baabs, (1991). New age fundamentalism. In C. Zweig & J. Abrams, eds., *Meeting the Shadow: The hidden power of the dark side of human nature* (pp. 160–161). Los Angeles: Tarcher.

Bataille, G. (1973). *Literature and evil.* London: Calder & Boyers.

Buber, M. (1964). *Daniel: Dialogues on realization* (M. Friedman, trans.). New York: Holt, Rinehart, & Winston.

———(1965). *Between man and man.* New York: Macmillan.

Buckley, P. (1981). Mystical experience and schizophrenia. *Schizophrenia Bulletin, 7,* (3), 516–521.

Butler, K. (1991). Encountering the shadow in Buddhist America. In C. Zweig and J. Abrams, eds., *Meeting the shadow: The hidden power of the dark side of human nature* (pp. 137–147). Los Angeles: Tarcher.

Carroll, N. (1990). *The philosophy of horror.* New York: Routledge.

Clarens, C. (1968). *An illustrated history of the horror film.* New York: Capricorn Books.

Freud, S. (1919/1958). The Uncanny. In Sigmund Freud, *On creativity and the unconscious* (pp. 122–161). New York: Harper & Row.

Friedman, M. (1964). *The worlds of existentialism.* Chicago: Random House/University of Chicago Press.

———(1991). *Encounter on the narrow ridge: A life of Martin Buber.* New York: Paragon House.

Gimbutas, M. (1989). *The language of the goddess.* New York: Harper & Row.

Grof, S. and C. Grof. (1989). *Spiritual emergency: When personal transformation becomes a crisis.* Los Angeles: Tarcher.

Hallie, P. (1969). *The paradox of cruelty.* Middletown, CT: Wesleyan University Press.

Hoeller, S. (1982). *The gnostic Jung and the seven sermons of the dead.* Wheaton, IL: Quest.

James, W. (1963). *Pragmatism and other essays.* New York: Washington Square Press. (Most of original work published in 1910.)

Jung, C. G. (1933). *Modern man in search of a soul.* New York: Harcourt, Brace, & World.

———(1961). *Memories, dreams, and reflections.* Ed. A. Jaffe, and trans. R. Winston and C. Winston. New York: Vintage.

Kaplan, B. (1964). *The inner world of mental Illness.* New York: Harper & Row.

Kaufmann, W. (1968). *Nietzsche: Philosopher, psychologist, antichrist.* New York: Vintage.

Kendrick, W. (1991). *The thrill of fear: 250 years of scary entertainment.* New York: Grove/Weidenfeld.

King, S. (1983). *Danse macabre.* New York: Berkeley Books.

Laing, R. D. (1967). *Politics of experience.* New York: Ballantine.

———(1969). *The divided self: An existential study in sanity and madness.* Middlesex, England: Penguin.

Leo, J. (1984, 8 October). The ups and downs of creativity: Genius and emotional disturbance are linked in a new study. *Time,* p. 76.

Leroux, G. (1911/1987). *The phantom of the opera.* New York: Signet.

Lifton, R. (1986). *The Nazi doctors.* New York: Basic.

Lukoff, D. (1988). Transpersonal perspectives on manic psychosis: Creative, visionary, and mystical states. *Journal of Transpersonal Psychology, 20,* (2), 111–139.

MacDonald, N. (1979). Living with schizophrenia. In D. Goleman and R. Davidson, eds., *Consciousness: Brain, states of awareness, and mysticism* (pp. 111–114). New York: Harper & Row.

140

Maslow, A. (1967). Neurosis as a failure of personal growth. *Humanitas, 3,* 153–169.

May, R. (1967). *Psychology and the human dilemma.* Princeton, NJ: Van Nostrand.

———(1969). *Love and will.* New York: Norton.

———(1985). *My quest for beauty.* Dallas, TX: Saybrook.

Morrow, L. (1991, 10 June). Evil. *Time,* pp. 48–53.

Moyers, B. (1988, 28 March). Interview with Raul Hilberg in Public Affairs television program, *Facing evil*—a conference sponsored by the Institute for the Humanities. *Journal graphics,* New York, NY. This typescript has also been published as a book: P. Woodruff and H. Wilmer, eds. (1988). *Facing Evil: light at the core of darkness.* La Salle, IL: Open Court.

Nietzsche, F. (1872/1956). *The Birth of tragedy and the genealogy of morals.* Trans. F. Golfing. New York: Doubleday/Anchor.

———(1886/1966). *Beyond good and evil.* Trans. W. Kaufmann. New York: Vintage.

Otto, R. (1923/1958). *The idea of the holy.* New York: Oxford University Press.

Poe, E. A. (1839/1981). The fall of the house of Usher. In *The complete Edgar Allan Poe tales* (pp. 199–212). New York: Chatham River Press.

Prentky, R. (1979). Creativity and psychopathology: A neurocognitive perspective. In B. Maher, ed., *Progress in experimental personality research* (pp. 1–39). New York: Academic Press.

Reese, W. (1980). *Dictionary of philosophy and religion: Eastern and western thought.* Atlantic Highlands, NJ: Humanities Press.

Richards, R. (1981). Relationships between creativity and psychopathology: An evaluation and interpretation of the evidence. *Genetic Psychology Monographs,* 103, 261–324.

Rifkin, J. (1983). *Algeny.* New York: Viking.

Rilke, R. M. (1982). *The selected poetry of Rainer Maria Rilke.* Trans. S. Mitchell. New York: Vintage.

Schneider, K. (1987). The deified self: A "centaur" response to Wilber and the transpersonal movement. *Journal of Humanis-*

tic Psychology, 27 (2) 196–216.

———(1989). Infallibility is so damn appealing: A reply to Ken Wilber. *Journal of Humanistic Psychology, 29* (4) 495–506.

———(1990). *The paradoxical self: Toward an understanding of our contradictory nature.* New York: Plenum/Insight.

Shapiro, D. (1965). *Neurotic styles.* New York: Basic.

Shelley, M. (1818/1981). *Frankenstein.* New York: Bantam.

Smith, H. (1986). *The religions of man.* New York: Harper & Row.

Stoker, B. (1897/1981). *Dracula.* New York: Bantam.

Styron, W. (1990). *Darkness visible.* New York: Vintage.

Tillich, P. (1952). *The courage to be.* New Haven, CT: Yale University Press.

———(1967). *My search for absolutes.* New York: Simon & Schuster.

Twain, M. (1962). *Letters from the earth.* New York: Harper & Row.

Twitchell, J. (1985). *Dreadful pleasures: An anatomy of modern horror.* New York: Oxford.

Webster's Dictionary (1968). *Webster's new world dictionary of the American language.* Cleveland: World Publishing Co.

Webster's Dictionary (1988). *Webster's ninth new collegiate dictionary.* Springfield, MA: Merriam-Webster.

Wood, R. (1969). *Hitchcock's films.* New York: Paperback Library.

Zweig, C. and J. Abrams (1991). *Meeting the shadow: The hidden power of the dark side of human nature.* Los Angeles: Tarcher.

Filmography (alphabetical listing of films discussed in the book)

Alien. (1979). Ridley Scott, Director. Twentieth Century-Fox (USA). Actors: Tom Skerritt (the Captain), Sigourney Weaver (Ripley), John Hurt (Kane), Ian Holm (Science Officer Ash), Yaphet Kotto, Harry Dean Stanton.

The Birds. (1963). Alfred Hitchcock, Director; Evan Hunter, Screenwriter; Daphne Du Maurier, Original Author. Universal (USA). Actors: Rod Taylor (Mitch), Tippi Hedren (Melanie), Jessica Tandy (Lydia), Suzanne Pleshette (Annie), Veronica Cartwright (Cathie).

Dr. Jekyll and Mr. Hyde. (1932). Rouben Mamoulian, Director; Samuel Hoffenstein and Percy Heath, Screenwriters; Robert Louis Stevenson, Original Author. Paramount (USA). Actors: Fredric March (Jekyll/Hyde), Miriam Hopkins (Ivy), Rose Hobart (Muriel), Holmes Herbert.

Dracula. (1931). Tod Browning, Director; Garrett Fort, Screenwriter; Bram Stoker, Original Author. Universal (USA). Actors: Bela Lugosi (Dracula), Helen Chandler (Mina), David Manners (Jonathan Harker), Dwight Frye (Renfield), Edward Van Sloan (Van Helsing).

The Fly. (1986). David Cronenberg, Director; Charles E. Pogue, Screenwriter. Twentieth Century-Fox (USA). Actors: Jeff Goldblum (Seth), Geena Davis, John Getz, Joy Boushel.

Forbidden Planet. (1956). Fred McLeod Wilcox, Director; Cyril Hume, Screenwriter. Metro-Goldwyn-Mayer (USA). Actors: Walter Pidgeon (Dr. Morbius), Ann Francis (Altaira), Leslie Nielsen (Captain Adams), Warren Stevens.

Frankenstein. (1931). James Whale, Director; Garret Fort, Francis E. Faragoh, Screenwriters; Mary Shelley, Original Author. Universal (USA). Colin Clive (Dr. Frankenstein), Mae Clark (Elizabeth), John Boles, Boris Karloff (the Monster), Edward Van Sloan, Dwight Frye.

Freaks. (1932). Tod Browning, Director; Willis Goldbeck, Leon Gordon, Screenwriters. Tod Robbins, Original Author. Metro-Goldwyn-Mayer (USA). Actors: Wallace Ford, Leila Hyams, Olga Baclanova, Roscoe Ates.

House of Usher. (1960). Roger Corman, Producer-Director; Richard Matheson, Screenwriter; Edgar Allan Poe, Original Author. American-International (USA). Actors: Vincent Price (Roderick Usher), Mark Damon (Philip Winthrop), Myrna Fahey (Madeline).

Incredible Shrinking Man. (1957). Jack Arnold, Producer; Albert Zugsmith, Screenwriter; Richard Matheson, Original Author. Universal (USA). Actors: Grant Williams (Carey), April Kent (Louise), Randy Stuart.

Invisible Man. (1933). James Whale, Director; R. C. Sherrif, Screenwriter. Universal (USA). Actors: Claude Rains (Dr. Griffin), Gloria Stewart (Flora), William Harrigan (Kemp), Henry Travers (Cranley).

Marnie. (1964). Alfred Hitchcock, Producer; Jay P. Allen, Screenwriter; Winston Graham, Original Author. Universal (USA). Actors: Tippie Hedren (Marnie), Sean Connery (Mark), Diane Baker, Martin Gabel, Louise Latham.

Phantom of the Opera. (1925). Rupert Julian, Producer; Carl Laemmle, Screenwriter; Gaston Leroux, Original Author. Universal (USA). Actors: Lon Chaney (the Phantom), Mary Philbin (Christine), Norman Kerry, Snitz Edwards, Gibson Gowland.

Psycho. (1960). Alfred Hitchcock, Producer; Joseph Stephano, Screenwriter; Robert Bloch, Original Author. Paramount (USA). Actors: Janet Leigh (Marion), Anthony Perkins (Norman), Vera Miles, John Gavin, Martin Balsam.

Rear Window. (1954). Alfred Hitchcock, Producer; John M. Hayes, Screenwriter; Cornell Woolrich, Original Author. Paramount (USA). Actors: James Stewart (L.B. Jefferies), Grace Kelly (Lisa), Wendell Corey, Thelma Ritter, Raymond Burr.

The Shining. (1980). Stanley Kubrick, Director; Stanley Kubrick and Diane Johnson, Screenwriters; Stephen King, Original Author. Warner Brothers (USA). Actors: Jack Nicholson (Jack), Shelley Duvall, Danny Lloyd, Scatman Crothers.

Vertigo. (1958). Alfred Hitchcock, Director; Alec Coppel and Samuel Taylor, Screenwriters; P. Boileau and T. Narcejac, Original Authors. Universal (USA). James Stewart (Scottie), Kim Novak (Madeline), Barbara Bel Geddes (Midge), Tom Helmore (Elster).

Index